The Jewish Community of Roman (Roman, Romania)

Translation of
Obstea evreiascaă din Roman

Published in Bucuresşti, 2001

This is a translation of: *Obstea evreiascaă din Roman*
(The Jewish Community of Roman), by Pincu Pascal
Published by Editura Hasefer, Bucuresşti, Romania, 2001

Published by JewishGen

**An Affiliate of the Museum of Jewish Heritage - A Living Memorial to the Holocaust
New York**

The Jewish Community of Roman
(Roman, Romania)
Translation of *Obstea evreiascaǎ din Roman*

Copyright © 2018 by JewishGen, Inc.
All rights reserved.
First Printing: November 2018, Kislev 5778
Second Printing: March 2019, Adar II 5779

Cover Design: Rachel Kolokoff Hopper
Editor: Yocheved Klausner
Translations by Sorin Goldenberg, Avishalom (Avi) Klammer,Emil Lax,
Rony Shaham & Monica Talmor
Editing and additional translations by Yocheved Klausner

Published by JewishGen, Inc.
An Affiliate of the Museum of Jewish Heritage
A Living Memorial to the Holocaust
36 Battery Place, New York, NY 10280

Printed in the United States of America by Lightning Source, Inc.

Library of Congress Control Number (LCCN): 2018963479
ISBN: 978-1-939561-70-1 (hard cover: 194 pages, alk. paper)

Cover Photo and Illustration: by Rachel Kolokoff Hopper

Cover Explanation: When I read *Obstea evreiascaă din Roman* to gather inspiration for the cover design, I was struck by two recurring themes in the book; the many synagogues of Roman and the horror of the death trains.

As in most European Jewish communities, places of worship were central to the lives of the Jews of Roman. By 1938 in Roman, in addition to the Great Synagogue (Sinagoga Mare) there were 16 other places of Jewish worship, most of them erected in the nineteenth century. It seemed only fitting that a synagogue should be central to the imagery for the cover for *Obstea evreiascaă din Roman.*

The second piece of imagery on the cover is a rail car used as part of a death train. Hundreds if not thousands of Jews died on the death trains and the trains are mentioned several times in *Obstea evreiascaă din Roman.*

An emotional historical account begins on page 84 of the book and describes the horror of the death train from Iaşi to Călăraşi which stopped in Roman as it passed through on July 2.

"Then, I saw what kind of inferno it was there, in a layer of human waste and blood, tens and tens of people in each wagon, naked, maddened by thirst, packed like sardines, the dead, the dying and the living all together. For three days they were traveling in an unbearable heat, in freight cars hermetically sealed, which had been used before to transport carbide. The smell was unbearable".

Many of the dead on that train were tossed from the cars in and near Roman and were later buried in the local Jewish cemetery.

On the cover, an old synagogue and a death train rail car are merged together to create a raw and visceral illustration as witness to the history of Roman. The image stands as a harsh reminder of the destruction of Jewish life in Roman and in all of Europe.

In this blended imagery, a wooden arched door of an old abandoned synagogue stands without support. We look through the arched door of the synagogue, a mainstay of the continuation of Jewish life in Roman and are startled and horrified to see a death train rail car.

The rest of the synagogue, beyond the arched doorway, all that remains of the walls and windows, are stretched across the landscape of the cover, like the ghosts of the Jews that once worshipped there.

The poem in the center of the back cover is by Max (Marcel) Blecher, a writer and poet from Roman. His words speak to the horror that his community endured. In his few simple phrases we are witness to the river of blood that was Roman and we feel the pain, loss, and longing for a life that is no more.

I hope this cover evokes a visceral emotional response for the vanished Jewish community and people of Roman. We cannot forget.

Never again.

JewishGen and the Yizkor-Books-in-Print Project

This book has been published by the **Yizkor-Books-in-Print Project,** as part of the **Yizkor Book Project** of **JewishGen, Inc**.

JewishGen, Inc. is a non-profit organization founded in 1987 as a resource for Jewish genealogy. Its website [www.jewishgen.org] serves as an international clearinghouse and resource center to assist individuals who are researching the history of their Jewish families and the places where they lived. JewishGen provides databases, facilitates discussion groups, and coordinates projects relating to Jewish genealogy and the history of the Jewish people. In 2003, JewishGen became an affiliate of the **Museum of Jewish Heritage - A Living Memorial to the Holocaust** in New York.

The **JewishGen Yizkor Book Project** was organized to make more widely known the existence of Yizkor (Memorial) Books written by survivors and former residents of various Jewish communities throughout the world. Later, volunteers connected to the different destroyed communities began cooperating to have these books translated from the original language— usually Hebrew or Yiddish—into English, thus enabling a wider audience to have access to the valuable information contained within them. As each chapter of these books was translated, it was posted on the JewishGen website and made available to the general public.

The **Yizkor-Books-in-Print Project** began in 2011 as an initiative to print and publish Yizkor Books that had been fully translated, so that hard copies would be available for purchase by the descendants of these communities and also by scholars, universities, synagogues, libraries, and museums.

These Yizkor books have been produced almost entirely through the volunteer effort of researchers from around the world, assisted by donations from private individuals. The books are printed and sold at near cost, so as to make them as affordable as possible. Our goal is to make this important genre of Jewish literature and history available in English in book form, so that people can have the personal histories of their ancestral towns on their bookshelves for themselves and for their children and grandchildren.

A list of all published translated Yizkor Books in the project with prices and ordering information can be found at:
http://www.jewishgen.org/Yizkor/ybip.html

Lance Ackerfeld, Yizkor Book Project Manager

Joel Alpert, Yizkor-Book-in-Print Project Coordinator

JewishGen
Yizkor Book Project

This book is presented by the
Yizkor Books in Print Project
Project Coordinator: Joel Alpert

Part of the
Yizkor Books Project of JewishGen, Inc.
Project Manager: Lance Ackerfeld

These books have been produced solely through volunteer effort
of individuals from around the world. The books are printed and
sold at near cost, so as to make them as affordable as possible.

Our goal is to make this history and important genre of Jewish
literature available in English in book form so that people can have
the near-personal histories of their ancestral towns on their bookshelves for themselves and for their children and grandchildren.

Any donations to the Yizkor Books Project are appreciated.

Please send donations to:
Yizkor Book Project
JewishGen
36 Battery Place
New York, NY 10280

JewishGen, Inc. is an affiliate of the
Museum of Jewish Heritage
A Living Memorial to the Holocaust

Acknowledgements

Our sincere appreciation to Alexandru Singer, Director of Editura Hasefer, for permission to use this material by JewishGen.

Geopolitical Information:

Roman, Romania: 46°55' N, 26°55' E

Alternate names for the town are: Roman [Romanian], Romesmarkt [German], Románvásár [Hungarian], Romanvarasch

Period	Town	District	Province	Country
Before WWI (c. 1900):	Roman	Roman	Moldavid	Romania
Between the wars (c. 1930):	Roman	Roman	Moldavid	Romania
After WWII (c. 1950):	Roman			Romania
Today (c. 2000):	Roman			Romania

Yiddish: ראמאן
In central Moldavia, 36 miles WSW of Iaşi, 28 miles E of Piatra Neamţ, 24 miles N of Bacău.

Jewish Population in 1900: 6,432 (in 1899), 5,963 (in 1930)

Nearby Jewish Communities

Budeşti 11 miles W
Bozienii de Sus 12 miles WNW
Dămieneşti 13 miles SSE
Băceşti 16 miles ESE
Buhuşi 17 miles SW
Roznov 20 miles WSW
Târgu Frumos 20 miles N
Plopana 21 miles SE
Bacău 24 miles S

Paşcani 25 miles NNW
Pungeşti 25 miles SE
Negreşti 25 miles ESE
Sîrca 25 miles NNE
Tazlău 25 miles SW
Podu Iloaiei 26 miles NE
Moţca 27 miles NNW
Izvoru Berheciului 27 mi SSE
Piatra Neamţ 28 miles W

UKRAINE

PODU
ILOAIEI ●

MOLDOVA

HUNGARY

IASI ●

ROMAN ●

BACAU ●

0 25 50 75 100 km

0 25 50 mi

ROMANIA

● BUCHAREST

SERBIA

Map of Romania with location of Roman indicated

Notes to the Reader:

Within the text the reader will note "{34}" standing ahead of a paragraph. This indicates that the material translated below was on page 34 of the original book. However, when a paragraph was split between two pages in the original book, the marker is placed in this book after the end of the paragraph for ease of reading.

Also please note that all references within the text of the book to page numbers, refer to the page numbers of the original Yizkor Book.

In order to obtain a list of all Shoah victims from Roman, the reader should access the Yad Vashem web site listed below; one can also search for specific family names using family name option. These lists are continually updated by Yad Vashem, so it is worthwhile to periodically search these lists.

There is much valuable information available on this web site, including the Pages of Testimony, etc.

http://yvng.yadvashem.org

A list of this book and all books available in the Yizkor-Book-In-Print Project along with prices is available at:

http://www.jewishgen.org/Yizkor/ybip.html

Summary

The Romanian city of Roman is situated in the northeastern part of the country, at the confluence of the Moldova and Siret rivers, on the great road of the Siret, which long ago connected the north of Moldova with the Danube ports. The Jewish population in the city is believed to date from as early as the beginning of 15th century. It is believed that a wooden synagogue existed in Roman at that time, on the same lot where the Main Synagogue was standing later (in the 20th century). It was but the first of what would become 18 synagogues serving a population of more than 6,000 Jews by the beginning of the 1940s, which along with a wide range of social, educational, and cultural institutions was a measure of the vitality of the community.

In this scholarly volume, the rich portrait of the Jewish community in Roman that was about to be annihilated is painted in meticulous detail, covering every aspect of life over the centuries of its existence.

Donni Magid

Table of Contents

Roman, Romania Yizkor Book

Family Notes

[Page 7]

A.

The Demographic Development of the Jews of Roman and Surroundings

Their Participation in the Economic, Cultural and Political Life. Aspects of Their Relationship With the General Population.

I. Jewish Presence in Roman and Surroundings Prior to 1938

The City of Roman is situated at the confluence of the Moldova and Siret rivers, on the great road of the Siret, which connected long ago the north of Moldova with the Danube ports. Roman is mentioned in "The List of Romanian Cities" compiled between 1287 and 1392, which indicates that the City existed even earlier. This is also based on the fact that the city seal is written in Latin, as well as the fact that according to Armenian traditions in Roman their first wooden church was purchased from the Sas ethnic group, in 1355. The ruler of Moldova, Roman Vodă Mushat, is the founder of the castle of Roman, as is mentioned in 1392[1].

With respect to the length of time of the presence of Jews in the city, there exist the following documents and evidence:

In the book of gold of the Community "Pinkas" [Register], dated 1773, there is an inscription from that year. In subsequent inscriptions it is mentioned that the old cemetery in 1872, when it stopped functioning, was 300 years old.

[Page 8]

Rabbi Iacov Isachsohn avers that he had seen, in 1880, a headstone of similar age.

A document of 1526 estopped Armenians and "Jews" trading in food and beverages, to prevent "contamination of Christians". From this document it is deduced that Jews started to settle in Moldova under the rule of Alexandru the Good, at the same time as the Armenians. "Strongly we urge all foreigners,

Armenians and Jews, to work industriously at the taverns, the food markets and the bakeries".[2]

A ruler's decree dated 29 November, 1825, by Ioan Sandu Sturza, regarding the old cemetery, concerning complaints of certain citizens of the City, avers that said cemetery was located there for "hundreds of years", there was no marketplace there, but "open space" and it is added "since even now it is not located in the middle of the town but far from it".

The correspondence of Stavrri with the famous Hagi Constantin POP from Sibiu asserts the existence of shop booths "of Bercu the Jew, near the bishopric, donated by Andronachi".[3]

Tradition supplements the documentation.

One of these holds that at the beginning of the XVth century there existed a wooden synagogue, situated on the spot of the actual Central Synagogue. At that time, Alexadru the Good, leaving for battle, directed that the Jews should pray for his victory and in fact he joined in the services held in the synagogue. After victory, the Ruler exempted the Jews from levies for three years.

[Page 9]

Another tradition holds that Bogdan Vodă the Blind, son of Stefan the Great, passing through Roman, Suceava bound, visited the wooden synagogue, donating a sum of money, with which a Torah scroll was brought from Poland, and it was known as the "Torah of Bogdan Vodă".

This holy writing existed till 1830, when the synagogue was set afire by the nobleman Vâlcov, when the Torah was burned as well. J. Kafman states in the "Israelite Magazine" that, in the year 1880, there were elders in Roman who said that they read from that Torah and gave precise details thereof.

In 1657, April 11, at Iaşi, Toader Banta made a complaint regarding a plot of land for a home, bought on the border of the town Scheia–Roman. A witness at the transaction was Moise, a Jewish doctor. "And this transaction was concluded at our own free will in front of their highness Ion Prăjescul treasurer, and in front of Iordache manager of the town of Iaşi and in front of Moisă the doctor and in front of the priest Bele from the town of Scheia..."[4]

The same Moise the doctor purchased in 1662, September 15, in Iaşi, houses from Iorga Karaiane.[5]

Certainly, this doctor had connections with the Roman county; some authors figure him to be the same as Doctor Cohen, from Iaşi. (Not to be confused with his namesake at the end of the following century.)

For the beginning of the XVIIIth century, the learned Bishop Melchisedec offers details regarding the Jews, beginning with the year 1704. But in detail, the documents of the Bishopric remind us of the rulers' book of 1709, wherein it stated that "it is owed to the Bishopric 2 bani per shop booth, all merchants from Roman–Christians, Armenians or Jews."[6]

[Page 10]

A tombstone discovered in 1928, when the construction of the "Roman Vodă" high–school began on the site of the cemetery, had the following content: "The Rabbi, our most devout tzadik and renowned for his distinguished qualities, David Ber, deceased on the 27th Tevet 5584 (1724)."[7]

In a book of court records from 1742, among the Jews of Iaşi, Isac and Volea, there is mention of a Jew from Roman, Haim.[8]

In 1745, a tombstone is mentioned, belonging to "the notable man, learned and teacher of laws, Mister Yehuda Leib son of Mister Tzvi Hersh.[9]

In 1785, CERBU, a "Jew from Roman" lived in Iaşi on Main Street, also known as the Squire's Street, litigated 12 years ago with Pavel the carter because of a bull drowned while pulling a cart with wine from Movilău.[10]

Similar transaction was done by Moise who brought a load from Ozarniţa to Roman, one.[11]

In 1765, the Jewish Community in Roman was wrongfully accused of plundering a church, they suffered insults and beatings.[12]

According to a document of the squires of 1769 only at the towns of Cernăuti, Botosani, Roman, Focsani, Galati, Chisinău there are settled shopkeepers". In Roman there was in 1794 a guild of Jewish craftsmen tailors.[13]

[Page 11]

According to the 1774 census there existed in Roman 14 Jewish families.[14]. P. Răşcanu mentions also two years later Jewish shopkeepers in the city.[15]

In 1780, on a list of debtors of the Squire Constantin Balş the following are recorded:

Solomon son of Cerbu, Lupu the Jew, Leiba the Gabbai (synagogue manager) of Jews, Lepu and Dov Focshaneanu, Litman the Jew, Giacal (who pawned pearls), Peisală Leibi Ishlicary's wife (made squire hats) and David son of Leibi, from Roman and Bercu the Jew for the feudal system from Trifesti, Pascal from Trifesti.[16]

In 1792, The Roman Bishopric owed to: Leiba "the Jew of Roman" 1053 lei and 99 bani, since 1786–August 25, but 1000 lei given in money and the balance merchandise, thus the 1000 lei accrued interest for 6 years and 2 months–493 lei and 40 bani; 413 lei and 33 bani to Leiba the short one and 224 lei to Smilu Barohu, the Jew.[17]

In the same year, Antoniu, Bishop of Roman, gave a plot of land for a house to doctor Moise, for definitely settling in town, "as to one who served the town and continues to serve it now". The document describes him as being "diligent and dedicated in the time of need, he sought out those who fell ill among the people".

The house was given to him on Main Street, to set up shop.[18] According to Dr. Epifanie Cozărăscu, the Precista Monastery Hospital, established in the city in 1798, if he were a full doctor with title, he would have been employed by the hospital; but he was not. Our query: was he still alive in that year?[19]

[Page 12]

According to M. Schwarzfeld, in 1794, at Roman the Jewish craftsmen's guild, which encompassed all without differentiating by discipline or specialty, decided to donate 2 lei yearly each to the Holy Society (probably the burial society *Chevra Kadisha*).[20]

Two years later, a document mentions "the shop booths of Bercu the Jew". [[21] In 1798, in the ledger of expenses of a certain glassware manufacturer from Miclăuşeni, Roman county, the following is recorded: Avram son of Iacob the craftsman, who received 70 lei for work (probably the same as Avram the Jewish glassblower mentioned in a document from 1785 in *Anuarului Eparhiei Romanului*, 1936), and Herşil who supplied potash ash (62 lei and 60 bani for 100 *merțe*). To the master they also gave at marriage time, 14 lei, money for meat, corn, wheat, and food. For two years of work he was paid 80 ducats.[22]

In the same year, the Ruler of Moldova, Alexandru Callimachi, regulated the rights of the Bishopric of Roman over the town and townspeople: for all the wine and brandy that will be sold in the town taverns, Christians, Jews and others will have to pay to the Bishopric 2 bani per a quantity of wine...and one ban for a quantity of brandy; but the sale will belong to the bishopric. Shopkeepers will pay also to the bishopric, for the site of the shop booth.[23] These levies being oppressive, the inhabitants of the city were against said liens. It was attempted to justify the increased dues by the building of the hospital, which required extensive funds.

N. Iorga offers us certain information regarding the Jewish trade in Moldova:

[Page 13]

"The Jews brought in their shop booths at fairs, foreign made merchandise – Turkish textiles, household utensils, tools for field workers from Graz, in Silezia...thick English cloth at convenient prices, and later all that was necessary to furnish a house according to European taste".[24]

Toward the end of the XVIIIth century, the Jews were involved in commerce and crafts: glassblower, doctor, tavern keepers, money changers. We must remember of course also the money changer Constantin Balsh, who was a titled squire. As a rule, the exchangers were those who had liquid currency.

In 1817, the inhabitants of the Scheia village complained of the leaseholder of the estate who subleased to Leiba the Jew the license for beverages. But over 4 decades the inhabitants of the Săbăoani estate, Roman County, complain also against the owner of the estate, Dimitrie Stan.[25] It is not the fault of any one nation, but of the lack of regulations in the fiscal, agricultural, etc. areas.

Statistics of the Jews in the 19th Century

The census of 1820 shows 104 Jews (families) that have been permitted to settle, while the one of 1832 shows 1154 Jews (see appendices). For the year of 1848 we have only civil records figures: born – 36, married – 10, and 20 deceased (12 men and 8 women[26]). Two years later, 363 Jewish families lived in the city[27], while other sources specify 562 Jews (families); otherwise we cannot explain the drastic reduction in numbers compared to the 1832 statistics.[28]

[Page 14]

Although the prince Mihail Grigore Sturza applied restrictive measures against the Jews, in the decree of 28 February 1844 he emphasizes:

Most of the towns in Moldova that are private property are inhabited by Jews, because the locals are much better suited to agriculture work.

If the Jews of these towns were forbidden to deal in food and drink commerce, there is no doubt that they, lacking the opportunity to earn their living, will leave the towns, which will remain deserted.

The consequences will be grave losses to properties, because there is no possibility to inhabit those towns with peasants, given that the big estates are in demand of inhabitants.[29]

Here is the number of Jews in the other towns.[30]

In 1859 at Bozieni there were 176 Jews and 172 Romanians, in Dămieneşti 155 Jews, while in 1889–1890 in those towns and others, the distribution was as follows: Bozieni (1890) 500 Jews and 500 Romanians, at Băceşti – 453 Romanians and 474 Jews, at Dămieneşti – 170 Romanians and 154 Jews, at Băra – 195 Romanians and 245 Jews, and at Onişcani – 80 Romanians and 68 Jews.

In 1895 at Băra there were 407 inhabitants, most of them Jews, while in 1890 at Bozieni – 350 Jews[31].

For the 6th decade of the 19th century, I. Psantir gives the following data: Băceşti – 120 families, Dămieneşti – 12 families, and Băra – 30 families[32].

For the year 1884, I Valentinianu presents the following statistics for Roman: births – Romanians 252 and Jews 312, deaths – 280 Romanians and 152 Jews.[33]

The great number of deaths in the Romanian population, especially in the villages, was explained – at the national level by Dr. Iacob Felix and at the local level by dr. Dimitrie Cantemir – by the lack of sanitarian assistance, and even more by the lack of social aid, which always was an important part of the budget of any Jewish community.

For the last half year of the year 1886, the local newspaper "Romanu" supplies us the following data: Romanians – births 262, marriages 45, deaths 203; Jews – births 136, marriages – 20, deaths – 75[34]. In 1887 there were 2116 Jews in the Roman County[35]. In the first trimester of that year 141 Romanians were born, 12 married and 138 deceased. In the same period, 70 Jews were born, 2 married, 38 deceased[36]. The next year, for the last trimesters, the situation was similar. Between 1 Aug 1887 – 1 Aug 1888, 559 Romanians were born, 70 married, and 479 deceased. 275 Jews were born, 18 married and 162 deceased[37].

For the year 1887 in the "United Plases" (Plasa – a subdivision of a county) there were 511 Jews of a total of 42,079 inhabitants, in Plasa Siretul de sus

(Upper Siret) 681 Jews of a total of 25,773 inhabitants, while in Plasa Fundul, 924 Jews of a total of 18,434 inhabitants[38]. In 1892, the number of Jews was 6025, compared to 7,182 Romanians[39]. In December 1894, there were in the city of Roman 6200 Jews (3134 men and 3,066 women), and in the county 7942 (3975 men and 3967 women)[40]. The total number of inhabitants in the county was 108,704 people.

[Page 16]

In 1831, the inhabitants of the city Roman have complained to the authorities, asking for the liquidation of the small alcohol distilleries, most of them kept by Jews, since, as mentioned in a document from 1846, some of the Jews have obtained various jobs at the big estates, renting distilleries, mills and forests[41].

In 1835, the under–physician Abraham Meizels, of 33 years age, a Jew from Bacău, is mentioned as the temporary replacement of the physician Alexandru Theodori; he spoke the Moldovan language. It should be mentioned that Dr. Theodori was responsible for the sanitarian services of the counties Roman, Bacău, and Neamţ, being a resident of Roman[42].

Various documents mention Leib, the money–lender, who lent 500 ducats to a certain boyar, as one of the shopkeepers – Haim Argintaru, David Argintaru, Iancu and Avram[43]. In 1852, Th. Codrescu mentions the merchants Hascal son of Iosip, Iţic Nadler, and the tailor Bercu. According to the newspaperman Marius Mircu, in 1831 there were 175 Jewish tailors.[44] The names of some of the synagogues refer to the occupations of the praying people: tailors, boot–makers, cabmen, etc.

Toward the end of the 19th century, the following merchants and craftsmen are mentioned: M. Berman – upholsterer (had also a furniture shop), Iosef Ratimberg, tannery, M. Bring – owned a shop selling "exotic goods" (spices, coffee, etc...), Uşer Vaisman – metal goods shop, Iosef Bainglas – tinsmith, had a glass and porcelain shop, Haim Solomon – bakery, Iosef Zingher – selling harnesses and money lender, Ioil Medonick, selling glass products, porcelain and tin products, M. Daniel – supplier of wood for heating[45]. Iosub Zingher manufactured soap and candles, while Leizer son of Nuhem had a mill with two stones[46].

A bigger factory, of leather goods, belonged to Grinberg.[47] Another who is mentioned is Sender Baraf, responsible of measurements accuracy, and E.

Rostreich who sold an uncommon product, lye for washing cows, extracted from tobacco.[48]

In general, the Jews of Roman have arrived, at different times, from Poland. In order to fill the unknown details about their origin, or the Romanian localities they lived before moving to Roman, we use the family names. The ones living in Roman for a long time are called ot Roman, mi (from in Hebrew) Roman, and those who had come recently Romaşcanu. We find others, as Iosăp a Jew ot Hălăucești, Haim Gălăţeanu, Sender Burdujanu, Heis Bârlădeanu, Iancu Horodniceanu, Sache Alterescu – Buz(o)ianu, Iancu Pietrenu, A. Polak (the Polish) etc.

[Page 18]

The family names help us identify their occupations as well: Zalman Stoleru (carpenter), Avram Ceasornicaru (watchmaker), Iţic Curelaru (harness maker), Max Blecher (tinsmith), Sandu Sticlaru (glass–maker), Iţic Cotiugaru (carriage driver), L. Tejghetaru (cashier), Pascal Bacal (grocer), Avram Meşter (craftsman).

There are those who carry usual Yiddish names, derived from German, others have translated their names to Romanian, as Cerbu (Hirsch–deer); others Romanized the Yiddish names – Alter – Alterescu. There are those who carry Romanian nicknames: Lungu (the long one), Scurtu (the short one), etc.

N. Iorga mentions that in the second half of the 19th century, the Englishman W. Beatty Kingston describes the city: "If among the three and half millions of the people in London, two millions were strangers, with criticizable habits, and all of the commerce was in their hands, I don't think the other one million and half would sympathize them" He declared this, thinking that in the city of Roman the Jewish element is dominant and that Roman can be compared with London[49]. The Englishmen though, have not been scared too much by the Jews, the proof being the lord Beaconsfield–Disraeli, who held the position of prime minister of the United Kingdom for a record–time, even though in that country the number of Jews was below the 4%, the maximal number achieved by Jews in Romania.

Following is the description of a German: "Inside, it (the town) resembles the other Moldovan towns, a long alley by the name of Uliţa Mare (the long alley), a row of open booths, covered carelessly, behind them standing some Jews dressed in black, with curly side–locks, or bearded Romanians in their sheep–hide coats... In the booths we find brooms, wooden articles, pots and pans, or food – in such small quantities that the worth of such a booth is hardly several golden coins."

[Page 19]

In the Romanian war of independence, Jews of Roman have fought alongside the Romanians. The soldier Froim Trent of the 14th infantry regiment died in the line of duty. Jews from the Roman city and county have contributed in money, food, animals and other objects. Some of them are enumerated in M. O. 22 Sep 1877, 6/18 Oct. 1877, 8/20 Oct. 1877, 22 Jan 1878 etc.

Performing their duties, the Jews thought they were entitled to rights. Thus, in the issue of 16 December 1878, the newspaper "Telegraful" published an impressive letter addressed to the president and members of the Romanian Parliament, requesting civil rights. They did not receive a positive reply.

Later, in 1880 and 1881, such rights were bestowed upon three Jews of Roman: Sache Alterescu, Ph.D. in law, awarded by royal decree the title of Knight of the order "Romanian Crown", the banker Ios. Moscovici and the pharmacist Max Frankel (M.O. 40/1880, 61/1880, 15/1881).

In 1885, the requests for citizenship of the Jews Aron S. Goldentahl, I. Reinstein, Feldman Simo, and E.L. Fischler were rejected[51].

In the 20th century, the demographic situation of the Jews in Roman and the neighborhood was the following: In 1900 there were 7982 Jews in the city, of which 3936 men and 4046 women[52].

[Page 20]

The most complete statistics is presented by Leonida Colescu, who gives the following numbers: in the Roman County there were 7.4% Jews, in the city of Roman there were 6432 Jews out of a population of 16288 inhabitants. In the rural communities, where Jews were less numerous, the number was 1804 out of 95300. At Băceşti there were 40, Băra 308, Dămieneşti 194, Galbeni 59, and Onişcani 44[53].

In 1905, based on the local community statistics, in the city there were 1027 family heads, 4620 people, 986 married men, 986 married women, widows 94, bachelors 17, widowers 23, boys at school age 1215, girls 1300, literate men 759 and literate women 453[54].

In 1912, there were 11754 Romanians in the city, and 5299 Jews; of other nationalities, there were 1075 inhabitants[55]. In 1925 dr. W. Filderman repeats those numbers. In 1926, Rabbi Mendel Frankel informs of 1000

Jewish families, with 3600 people. In 1930, there were in the city 7129 Jews, in 1939 – 7163, in 1941 – 6025, and in 1942 – 6485 (24.8%)[56]. In that year there were 4639 literate Jews (78.3%).

One of the Jewish occupations was tenant (land leaser). There are also mentioned associations of tenants. Thus, in 1859 the Jews Ariton Solomon, Hascal and Cunea son of Iosip, form such an association[57]. In that time, also existed the tenant trusts of the families Costiner, Iuster, and Gutman[58]. Based on other data, Jews held in the 20th century in the Roman County: 706 ha. of arable land, 300 ha. of grazing land, 1454 ha. of forests, 2460 ha. in total.

[Page 21]

In 1907, the demands of all the peasants were the same: reduction in the prices of leasing the plowing fields and the grazing fields, and correct accounting. Everywhere, the houses of the tenants were destroyed, the accounting registers torn, the clerks beaten.

A newspaper of that time remarks that in Moldova "most of the tenants are Jews. In order to transform the agrarian revolt into a pogrom, all that was needed was several clever maneuvers; all that was required was the intervention of the clever anti–Semitic demagogy, the kind we find so disgraceful, all over Europe"[59].

The socialists and the students exploited this and, based on the existence of an anti–Semitic wave, were trying to give it a religious aspect. Beccaria, an Italian diplomat, mentions the Fischer trust in Moldova, which possessed 237000 ha. of leased land, of those 159000 ha. arable land. The tenants paid 21 lei per hectare, and demanded of the peasants 40–60 lei per hectare.

Following Beccaria, the one who was to blame was the government, who tolerated the existence of Jewish trusts for leasing land, although it was illegal by law[60].

At Hălăuceşti, the shop of a Jewish woman was destroyed, and at Muncel, the bureau of Milo Somer. In the same village, on 12 March the peasants of the village, together with those of Mogoşeşti, destroyed the Jewish shops. At Trifeşti, Herzberg's courtyard was destroyed. The inn–keeper Aron, being attacked, has defended himself, together with his son, until the army arrived[61]. Radu Rosetti affirms that not only Jewish houses were destroyed, the fact being confirmed by documents.

[Page 22]

Violence occurred in the communities of Herbăşeşti, Strunga, Criveşti, and Brătuleşti, where 400 peasants went through the communities, driving the Jews away. The shop of the merchant Iacobsohn was ruined, and the merchandise thrown out in the street.[62] The peasants of Bârjoveni kept the brothers Solomon, tenants, captive, demanding the abolition of debts[63]. Severe clashes occurred in the community Cârligi, where the estate of the brothers Zarifopol, was leased by I. Spotheim. "The revolt had a very violent character; the peasants sought to kill the tenant, and destroyed his house. Although the landowner Zaripofol has promised to change the arrangements, the peasants held to their threatening attitude, requiring the prefect to send troops from the 8th artillery regiment".[64].

Although the Jews of Roman have participated in the Romanian war of independence, and the grant of civil rights was denied, they still kept fighting for the country where they were born.

During the Bulgarian campaign in 1913, the soldier from Roman Cahane Leibu, of the 14th infantry regiment, died. Three years later, Romania joined WWI, called the war for the union of the nation. The Jews of course, participated in this war as well.

The city and County of Roman has sacrificed many victims during this war. Among them 19 dead, 14 wounded, 7 heroes were decorated. The following died during the fights: Baum Max, soldier of the 16th infantry regiment, Bercovici Iancu, Coflea Herşcu, Chegler Wolf, David Strul, A. Edelstein, Ellman Iancu, B. Feldstein, Galet Iţic, Katz N. Bercu, Moses Avram, Meer Nuţă, Scorţanu Leiba, Å¢ifui Isac and Zait Gavril, soldiers of the same regiment. Others that died were T.R. Chegler Å¢alic, Leizer Manole and Leiba Mendel (maintenance corps). The following soldiers of the 16th infantry regiment were wounded: Cherpel Haim, Feler Herşcu, Handel Frederic, Haimovici Faibiş, Marcu Ilie, Marcu Iacob, Romanaşcanu Moise, Sfarţ Lazăr, and the officer Adm. Israil Gh.

[Page 23]

The following were decorated: Atlasman Lazăr (soldier of the 16th infantry regiment) with "Manhood and Belief" with swords, 3rd class. From the same regiment, the following have received the same decoration: Leibovici Aron, Meer Vigder, Roşu Ilie, and Sacaleţ Herşcu. The soldier Rivenzon David has been decorated with 2nd class[66].

The constitution of 1923 granted the Jews civil rights. The U.E.R (Union of Romanian Jews) has conducted a bitter struggle for obtaining those rights.

In 1934, the Jews of Roman have celebrated 15 years since emancipation. The mayor of the city, Moisina, participated in the festivity along with the Jewish representatives, pharmacist Horovitz and the lawyer Schwartz[67].

We have only limited information about the participation of Roman Jews in local politics. In 1926, the following were candidates on the Liberal list: Iancu Gross, lawyer N. Maximilian Schor, Osias Beram, H. Haimovici, and Bercu Zingher[68].

In the 20th century, the fields of occupation of the Roman Jews diversified.

[Page 24]

New professions appeared among Jews, and in the practiced professions their number increased.

In the jubilee exhibition of 1906, some Jews from the Roman County were awarded prizes. M. Somer–Poiana (for wheat), A. Focşaner–Cordun (the same), both receiving bronze medals with a special diploma, and Leizer Rubel–Trifeşti, I. Spodheim–Cârligi (corn), R. Cligher–Oniceni (barley), Oscar Guttman–Boteşti (beans and barley), Ackerman–Stăniţă (wheat), B. Zingher Băceşti (wheat), A. Focşaner–Cordun (wheat), C. Iacobsohn–Strunga (rye), N. Isac–Tupilaţi (barley), were awarded diplomas and special distinction.[69]

In 1936, the firms S.I.N.C – David Laufer and M. Zingher of Roman, were mentioned for commerce of cereals and their derivates, with a capital of 500000 lei, and S.A. "Prodagricol" Roman, for the industrialization and commercialization of agricultural products and derivates, with a capital of 1 million lei, invested by a group of seven people, among them M. Zingher – 350000 lei, B. Rohrlich – 300000 lei, and I. Brucmaier – 100000 lei.[70]

The appendices offer abundant material about the numbers and diversity of the commerce practiced by the Jews in the Roman town and County. Solomon Zingher was the president of the merchants' council in Roman, and A. Weisman was the president of the merchants' council in Băceşti-Roman.[71] In the 20th century the following workshops and factories existed in Roman: the leather factory "Zimbru" belonging to the Rosemberg brothers, with a capital of 5 million, the workshop of leather processing belonging to Isac and Iancu Mairsohn, S.I.N.C. with a capital of 100000 lei, the soap factory "Luceafărul" of Aron Margulis, with a capital of 150000 lei, the sweets and marmalade factory of H. Ghelberg and Gh. with a capital of 409000 lei, the factory of articles made of tin and metal–wire "Leul" of M. Saider, with a capital of 250000 lei, factory of metal–wire "Vulturul" belonging to Anita Lebovici, with a capital of 200000 lei, tin factory "Fierul" of Herman Kendler, with a capital of 150000 lei, the factory of articles made of metal–wire "Gloria" of Sigmund Rosen with a capital of 250000 lei, the foundry "Ferometal" of Avram Davidovici, with a capital of 200000 lei, the terracotta factory of Lazăr Blecher, with a capital of 300000 lei[72]. In his notes, the Rabbi Mendel Frenkel also mentions: the Rohrlich mill, the leather factory Grimberg, and several other workshops for manufacturing hairgrips, buckles, soap, candles. The archives material add also: the textile factory of Marcovici Silvian, the factory owners Mayersohn Buium, Max Bucă, Stein Iosif, Moses Schechter, Werner Solomon, Iosub Leizerovici, the cinema owner I. Lazarovici, the harness work–shop I. Stumer, the oil factories Grimberg Samoil, Grimberg Adolf, Grimberg Moriț and Grimberg Iţic, the timber factory of Straucher Moriț, Straucher Vili and Straucher Iosif.[73]

[Page 25]

II. The Jews in Roman during the period of the Dictators

The short duration of the Goga–Cuza regime has left its imprint on the life of the Jews, particularly with respect to the problem of renewing their citizenship. This would continue with perseverance also under the Legionary government.

[Page 26]

From the correspondence of the community of Roman with "the Union of Communities of the Former Kingdom [*Regat*]", we discover that those without citizenship were divided into two categories:

Those reviewed and rejected. In order to obtain identity cards, they were asked to present their wedding certificates and their children's birth certificates, proof of having satisfied their military service and receipts of their taxes payments.

Those who were not reviewed or were not citizens, possessing: a travel document (if a foreigner), a Nansen passport (if Romanian), birth certificates or military record. In 1939, there have been 101 Jews without Romanian citizenship[74]

In general, the documents do not offer us any real data, but only the reflection of the characteristic events in the whole country at the time. There has not been any victim. The display windows and the doors of the Jewish stores were glued on with posters: "Attention! A Jidov's shop"! ["jidov"= a derogatory term for a Jew].[75]

The Pogrom in the city of Isai had profound connections with the Roman County. A certain document appears to lead to the idea of premeditated plans. A week prior to the arrival of the death trains, the Jews of Roman have dug communal graves for those who would die in the torturing "death trains."

Of the wanderings of such a train we find out also in the local newspaper "Ceahlăul" no. 107/16 VI 1990: In Mircești, the dead and the dying were thrown from the train cars, loaded onto carts requisitioned in advance and flung again, this time along the Northern part of the "Iugani Canal." There, as the heat waves were great, they have grown putrefied. Not able to breathe any more in town, the authorities have requisitioned carts again and by compulsory labor dug a common grave at the intersection of the communal road of Iugani and the National Road Pașcani–E–85.

[Page 27]

Professor Trifan asks: Are there one hundred? Hundreds? Ask yourselves, good Christians, if someone came to the assistance of the dying. Witnesses, who would not give their names, gave the excuse: fear of the town's Gendarmes! Anyone who would step out would be hit with the butts of their rifles, with special predilection toward dying Jews!

Nevertheless, it appears that at least one of the dying has been saved; it must have been the one who was hidden in the cellar of Mr. Dumitru Vernica, a Sergeant ctg. 1936 of Mircești. This probability arises from the fact that when Mr. Vernica died on December 30th, 1985, his spouse, not liking to boast, has related to us, nevertheless, that Mr. Vernica, while acting in the capacity of a provisions Sergeant with the Pioneers of the Cernăuți Unit, had saved the Jew Leizer Rosenthal, who subsequently succeeded in reaching the U.S.A.

A controversial fact is that of the obligation to wear the Yellow Star, at least for a limited time. Here is what Oliver Lustig is telling us in "The Flame" of 5–December–1986: "It is true that, through ordinance number 3/23. VIII. 1941, the General Constantin Cernătescu, commander of the 4th (VI) territorial headquarters, ordered that all residents of Jewish ethnic origin, of whichever sex or age, found in passage or residing in the judiciary territory of the 4th territorial headquarters (the counties of Iași, Baia, Botoșani, Roman, Soroca) are obliged, in 48 hours of the present announcement, to wear a distinctive mark on the left side, of two equilateral triangles of a 7–centimeter base, superposed in such a way so as to form the Jewish star, made of yellow cloth". It is right that over some time, it seems a month, this ordinance has been revoked. Although the city of Piatra Neamţ and the Neamţ County have not been part of the headquarters of the zealous general, the yellow star was worn there; among other similar testimonies, we should mention also that of Professor Ştefan Cazimir.

[Page 28]

With or without obvious reasons, there have been Jewish refugees from the towns and villages of the Roman County, as well as from Târgul Frumos and Târgul Neamţ. They ran from their homes leaving behind all their property and savings – hundreds of millions of Lei. Thus, on 11 July 1941, in Roman there were 807 people evacuated from the county, who did not have the means of providing for themselves sugar, oil and bread; 331 ate at a community kitchen while 476 obtained their food supply through commerce.[76]

In 1942, the city of Roman had 6,485 Jews including those from evacuated towns: Băceşti, Dămineşti, Bozieni, Negreşti. 64 Jews were deported to Transnistria, 1116 were taken to compulsory labor, 685 of them in the county and the rest in the city. Most of them received help: 270 had lunch at the canteen, 160 had at home lunch supplied by the canteen. They were not allowed to step out of their homes, stores or workshops except between the hours 10–12 a.m., the children were not allowed to leave their courtyards.[77]

[Page 29]

For the effectuation of compulsory labor, statistics regarding age have been drawn up. Among women born between the years 1889–1905, 789 have been selected for compulsory labor, while among those born between the years 1920–1929, 677 have been selected.[78]

Child labor constituted a particularly disturbing chapter. Thus, in an address of the "General Staff of the IVth Army Corps, office 9 Jews" to the county office C.E.R. Roman we read: "The Great General Staff by ordinance 433703/25.XII.1943 orders that Jews between the ages of 15–17 who perform compulsory labor in the local townships not be paid anything since they do not fall within the framework of those fit for labor ".

In the event of desertion, measures were taken against the parents. In a report regarding the work of teenagers of ages 15–17 in the Roman City Hall, we find out that: "from the date of 28 June 1943, 10–12 of the teenagers have been used as cart boys of the City Hall oxen cart for carrying garbage off the streets and carrying away the construction waste of the old courthouse.

– A group of 12 teenagers is working at cleaning the public gardens, sweeping and watering the parks and tending the flower beds.

– Another group is scrubbing the mosaic tile stones which function as border edges for sidewalks.

– Another group is turning the concrete mixers for footbridges (6–8 teenagers were assigned for each manual task).

[Page 30]

– Other groups are spreading construction waste on streets and sweeping the "non–asphalted" streets. Groups of teenagers gather the hay and make bales."

Starting on 20 August 1943, 15 teenagers worked at covering a trench shelter. Part of the teenagers removed old border edges from streets and replaced them with new ones. The work hours are 7–12, 14–18, sometimes extended. Many of the teenagers have been beaten by Pavel, the driver of the oxen cart, since, in his opinion, they were not well–trained to handle oxen and were not loading quickly enough the gravel, the sand, the dirt, the construction waste. Even the mayor has beaten teenagers.

The children, 160 in number, worked since 28 July 1943 with no rotation applied.

E. Popescu, the engineer who conducted the work of the teenagers (whose number the mayor had reduced on September 1st) dismissed those who did not satisfy the required workload conditions, those who were small in stature, the weak and the sick; he retained 30–40 better–developed teenagers.[79]

The F.C.E.R. archives contain documents which record the compulsory labor in the service of the Romanian national roads. From those documents the following emerged: the workers were subjected to hard labor, inadequate nutrition and mistreatment. The same conclusions can also be drawn from Leon Segal's memoir, which was dedicated to the Roman 450 Jews who have effectuated the compulsory labor in the service of the Romanian roads.

[Page 31]

Something about the work detachments:

– Dorohoi's detachment was divided into three groups: the first group was in Herța, the second in Vărnav and the third in Dorohoi. The Jews have been provided with travel assistance by the C.E.R. Roman County office.

– Detachment 8 roads, Company 5 quarry, established in the Lisa–Teleorman community. In November 1943 they went to Turnu Măgurele. The county C.E.R. Teleorman office reported that in the county, in Salcea near Roșiori de Vede, there was a detachment which included people from Roman; most of them were barefoot and naked.

Conforming to ordinance M. Statute M. number 928.265/942, Jews who were registered and those exempt from compulsory labor were obligated to contribute donations for equipping the exterior detachments. Those who would not contribute would be confined to a labor camp (the Ordinance of the Commander of the IVth Territorial Corps, Office 9, of December 12th).

Chief of General Staff   Chief of Office 9

C. Mironescu   Major Gogu[80]

On 25 April 1943, 133 Jews left for Sihna Botoșani; over 100 of them needed to be fitted out. From 15 May 1942, 250 Jews performed compulsory work in Florești–Bassarabia and 100 from September 1942. 35 craftsmen were concentrated in Tiraspol, and some of the Roman Jewish craftsmen were rounded up in Iași and Rădăuți.

350 Jews performed compulsory work in Florești and Măcin at a stone quarry. In June 1943, 600 of Roman's Jews were dispatched as exterior detachments.

[Page 32]

In Roman, 1143 Jews, 851 of them between the ages of 20–40, were mobilized as exterior detachments.

Local Detachments
The Army

Division 7	1
14th Regiment Infantry	37
4th Regiment Artillery	46
12th Regiment Cavalry	10
64th Regiment Artillery	17
3rd Battery Instr. Auto	19
Legion of Gendarmes	5
4th Company Sanitation	8
Subsistence storehouse (Depot)	C 4 A/7
Surrogate Military Factory	4
Roman's Territorial Group	2
Transport Service (Usually–food)	2
Military supply warehouse	6
Military hospital Z I/445	7
Precista Mare Hospital 448	13
Roman's Arms warehouse	6
The office of military zone	10
The firefighter's section	3
Trifeşti Ammunition	1
Total	204 Jews

Civilian Authorities

Roman City Hall 54; Communal enterprise 4; Industrial high school 12; Sugar factory 25; Boys high school 2

Total – 97 Jews

[Page 33]

Exterior Detachments

The Service of National Roads 137 Jews / Section L4 C.F.R. Bacău 23 Jews

Batalion 1 Roads Predeal 13 Jews / 8th Batallion Roads Roşiori de Vede 235

Batalion 4 Roads Predeal 1 Jew / Regiment 4 Pioneers, detachment 103 150 Jews

Company 5/7 Măcin 95 Jews / The Transnistrian Government 2 doctors

"Recuperation" barrack (infirmary) Tiraspol 30 Jews / The Transnistrian Government 1 pharmacist

Clothes manufacturing workshop Iaşi 3 Jews / Insurance House Petroşani 1 doctor

Prisoners' camp Independence 1 pharmacist

Instruction center Sarata 1 doctor / Garrison Predeal 1 doctor

Ghindinici Detachment 5 Jews / Livezeni Hunedoara detachment 1 doctor

Camp 6 Calafat 2 doctors

Total 726[81]

Mendel Cuperman and Moise Leibovici were released in Roman after having been detained for over 3 years in the country and in Transnistrian camps. Their families were short of living supplies. The sewing machine of Zaharia A. Şloim, a refugee and Gendarmes' Warrant Officer (Sergeant), was confiscated. These people were refugees from Târgul Frumos.[82]

The Jew Simon Ghingold's travel authorization was not released so he could not relocate to Iaşi. Concerning the acquirement of coats and jackets necessary for the Jews of the exterior detachments – the M.A.I orders have not provided for such a case.[83]

[Page 34]

In February 1943, a petition was addressed to the president of the county bureau of C.E.R. Roman, collections section, which reads: There is a total of 1143 mobilized Jews, out of which 851 Jews are today in the detachment of Măcin, Floreşti; in Tiraspol there are about 400 Jews.

For the rest of the Jews who will eventually be sent (in the Predeal detachment, 130 Jews) as well as for Jews from interior detachments, there would be need for equipment, shown in the adjoining table. To establish the necessary equipment specified in the table, we have taken as norm the percentage of Jews (50%) equipped by us for the exterior detachments, as would be the case with the Floreşti detachment, where the Jews were held for 10 months (with the exception of the legal leave and replacement of the sick) and those who worked in the stone quarry, where the clothing used is being torn quickly. The Jews in the Măcin detachment, who also worked in stone and are wearing out the equipment in a very short time, found themselves in the same situation. Out of a number of 283 Jews left in the interior detachments, there were about 150 Jews who needed to be equipped and for whom a special effort would be made in order to provide for their needs – an effort which would prove hard enough to actualize since, until the present two collections have been made for this purpose, which exceeded our city's means. In addition, an amount of 848,616 Lei was spent by the Roman Jewish community in aid for the Jews of the exterior detachments, as follows:

[Page 35]

Floreşti detachment: cash (244,220 Lei), medicines (54,549), food supply, cigarettes, tools (147,000 Lei).

Măcin detachment: cash (62,800 Lei), medicines (8,966 Lei), food supply and miscellaneous (27,869 Lei).

Bârlad detachment: cash (88,435 Lei), medicines (1045 Lei).

Dorohoi–Iaşi detachment: cash (46,425 Lei), medicines (19,334 Lei), food supply, cigarettes, miscellaneous (139,308 Lei).

Tiraspol detachment: cash (7,505 Lei).

Total: 848,617 Lei

Floreşti detachment: cash (244,220 Lei), medicines (54,549), food supply, cigarettes, tools (147,000 Lei).

There were also people who helped those suffering:

The assistance of Sir Samoil Hirsch concerns the Jews of the detachment Bucureşti, Saint Apostoli St.[84]

I have the honor to confirm the receipt of the packages sent by you personally and our compatriots who are in Bucureşti. Through your gesture, we shall alleviate the suffering of many needy families of the locality. We hope that in the future, you will honor us with the same attention and generosity, for which we are asking that you accept our thanks.

President   With particular honor
Leo Rohrlich   for the general secretary
                 Pharmacist J. Horowitz   (Personal archive Pincu Pascal)

[Page 36]

The sum of 500,000 lei was paid on October 1943 by five Jews for exemption from compulsory labor.[85]

However, S. Cristian affirms that Jews who possessed exemption cards have been taken into compulsory labor as well.[86]

In July 1944, 131 Jews discharged from the 678th German Pioneer battalion, who had been taken from the 52nd German Pioneer battalion, worked in 4th battalion–roads (5thcorps Army). The work was performed in the village Storneşti–Iaşi, 40 km from Roman, and the Roman Jewish community supplied them with food every five days. The men were housed in uncovered sheds; work conditions were inadequate. For about two months, Jews from the detachment were not given the possibility to bathe or to mend their clothes.[87]

In 1944, 1200 Jews were assigned to compulsory labor: 150 in the Teleorman detachment; 100 in the Cataloiu detachment; 120 in Oancea–Brăila; 60, in the C.F.R.–Bacău; 30 in the cavalry detachment and 300 in the exterior detachments.[88] The Jewish refugees from Târgul Frumos were assigned to the following detachments: Oţeleni 59, the 55th battalion P. Sagna 17; workshop 55; automobile 24[89]. In the same year, the following were assigned for work at the military detachments: 4th company, 2nd platoon Poeniţa 72; 1st Platoon Carol Gădinţi 103; 8th battalion roads 23; IV Company 3rd platoon Lucşa 48; the German Mission "antitank" 98.[90] In June 1944, the Jews were evacuated from Târgul Neamţ. In May 1944, the leading committee of the Târgul Frumos community was established and, owing to opposition to compulsory labor, the Jews were threatened with "ghetto–ization."[91]

[Page 37]

In 1940, the Hebrew school was confiscated. During the legionary period, attempts to "Romanianize" enterprises and buildings belonging to Jews were made. Later, the Ion Antonescu government successfully completed this plan.

In 1941, the Schwartz building on Dr. Riegler's St. was confiscated,[92] in 1942 the community building on 3 Miron Costin St. was passed to C.N.R; on 4 February 1943, 25 buildings belonging to the local community (hospital, old–age shelter, fowl slaughter–house, girls' primary school, soup kitchen, 13 synagogues and the cemetery) were "Romanianized". On 22 June 1943, the same happened with the property of the Băcești community (the synagogue and the bathhouse), and again, on 26 June 1943, with two more synagogues in Roman.[93] Agricultural property which was owned by Jews was expropriated: a total of 2,460 ha. (arable land, pastures, forests).[94]

Enormous sums of money were paid under pompous titles, such as lending for re–integration. Some authors cynically affirmed that the war has been conducted with the money of the Jews. Many times, the loser was the one found guilty. There have been indications of losses suffered by the Jews evacuated from towns and villages. Beds, mattresses, bed sheets, pillows, etc. have been confiscated.[95]

A sad chapter for Roman's Jews was the deportation to Transnistria. In September 1942, Jews suspected of Communism were sent there. Most of them have not had any connection with Communism and we don't know whether any ethnic Romanian Communist was deported there.

[Page 38]

Feinstein Jean, a chef from Roman was accused of having conducted, in 1921, subversive activities in the circle of the waiters' syndicate – a fact which was not proven in any court since it was not even examined.[96]

Sofia Marcovici of Roman (5 Petru Rareş St.), aged 64, presented a petition to Marshal Antonescu, in which we read:

"On 5 September 1942 my husband, Ilie Marcovici, aged 74 years, was sent to Vapniarka camp. At present he is in Grasulovca–Tiraspol. The commission found my husband innocent and placed his name on the list of those to be released. As the first phase of liberation took place in the Transnistria ghetto and my husband was ill and incapable of moving, he asked to remain in the camp's infirmary."[97]

Abramovici Marcu was in Mostovici–Berezovca (Transnistria), sent there in September 1942. He had never engaged in politics. Kirenman Marcu was in Berezovca, sent at the same time, was not accused of any political activity and has not asked for repatriation. Alter Iţic, sent to Transnistria in the same period, was equally not accused of political activity.[98] Lehrer Herman, having returned from there, was interned in the T.B.C. Bisericani Sanatorium.

Children were also sent to Transnistria, most of them repatriated in 1943. It was there that Tejgetaru Moise Leib was born.[99]

We must also mention the physicians, Dr. Micu and Falcoianu who tried to save a pregnant deportee.[100]

[Page 39]

For the collection of clothes for Transnistria & Dorohoi, the following commissions operated:

– Misses Toni Avram, Bella Iohan, Mr. Avram Iacob, Messrs. Maximilian Schor and Richard Stein (for Dorohoi).

– Miss. Charlotte Krakauer, Mrs. Sidonia Brand, Misses Roza Steinberg and Liza Feider, Messrs. Iosub Segal and Marcel Zingher.

– Messrs. Rudi Markus, Marcel Iancu, Zilman Feider, Avram Ghertner and Miss. Nahuma Solomon and Florica Koffler.

– Misses Fani Veidenfeld, Hermina Hirsch, Margareta Schwartz, Surica Pincu, Rebeca Pincu, Bella Veiss, Jeni Stein, Fani Horovitz and Messrs. David Schaechter, Solomon Sabo, Gherşin Moldoveanu, Gerşin Curelaru, Iosub Maier, Aizic Baier and the engineer Beer Camille.[101]

For the repatriation of 150 children from Transnistria in February 1944, there were the following delegates from Roman: Dr. Maier Reznic, Dr. Iosef Straucher, Dr. Leo Wiegler and Dr. Max Lazarovici.[102]

If all of those misfortunes took place owing to the times and laws, it did not mean that "there didn't exist particular initiatives, too".

In Roman, for example, it was the mayor N.C Pipa, of whom the rabbi Mendel Frankel wrote: "We should not forget the bestial behavior of the former mayor who has not permitted one Jew of the 53, buried in the Jewish cemetery of the locality, to be saved" (they were buried alive!).

The same mayor ordered that the Jews receive 200gr. of sugar a month per person while the gypsies were receiving 200gr. and the Christians 500gr.[103], considering that, in fact, gypsies too, are Christians. In February 1943, by the decision of the same mayor, Jews were allowed to procure food supply only after 10 a.m.; "those who would not respect this decision would be sent to (labor) camp."[104]

[Page 40]

In April 1944, the mayor became brutally involved in the affairs of the community, requesting the resignation of the committee, the new committee to be established by him.[105]

Ion Dascalescu, a refugee from Ardeal, complained to the ministry of health that the Roman sanitary service issued an authorization for the Jews, contrary to the law.[106]

But there was also Viorica Agarici, for whom I have reserved a special place.

[Page 41]

B. The Jewish Community of Roman throughout time

I. Historical evolution of the community of Roman

In his book, Professor S. Rivenzon mentions the famous and controversial megila (scroll of remembrance), found in the collection of Mr. M. Schwarzfeld, which narrates an episode that transpired at Roman in 1574, during the time of Ionaşcu Vodă Armeanul (Ion Vodă cel Cumplit). Famous experts in paleography who examined the document concluded that the megila was authentic. Jewish chroniclers, Mr. M. Schwarzfeld and later on Dr. M. A. Halevy, utilizing more adequate means of research and based on historical considerations deduced that it was an apocryphal masterpiece. Why would the author have chosen the city of Roman? Because Roman was one of the earliest cities inhabited by Jews in Moldova.[1]

The first leader of a Jewish community in town was Leiba, the "Staroste" of the Jews (1790) one of the debtors of Squire Constantin Balş.

In general, the Jewish Community (kahal) was engaged in operating schools, hospital, cemetery and other Jewish institutions, also being the representatives of the community in its relationship with other ethnicities among whom they dwelt.

[Page 42]

In Moldova, the community also was responsible to pay a levy on behalf of the Jews from that community. The leadership of the Jews of Roman was composed of 14 individuals who were involved in the running of the school, hospital, synagogues and cemetery.

They paid, in the times of Nicolae Suţu, a state tax of 60 (sixty) ducats, for 562 Jews; it is believed that it probably meant 562 heads of household.

Prior to N. Suţu, the amount paid as taxes by the Jewish community was unknown. This method of collective/communal payment (called **cisla**) was maintained till 1848, when a disposition of the rulers obligated all inhabitants to pay an individual levy. Yet, for Piatra Neamţ we have documentation of this collective taxation system in 1859. The community sustained the following positions: Rabbi, school teachers, hospital physician. The available documents reflect only a more recent listing of the officers of the Community of Roman, which functioned between 1870–1880, and was composed of: Lupu Davidovici, Ire Handman, Haim Jaller, Haim Gălăţeanu, David Abram.[2]

Documents from the end of the previous century show that "because of the disorganization of the Community and the internal conflicts, the maintenance of the hospital suffered, the bath was not built, and help to needy families was inadequate.[3]

The conflicts mentioned above arose between the students who wanted civil rights and assimilation on one side and the leadership of the community, conservative, opposed to assimilation, but not without arguments. The local authorities supported the community.[4]

[Page 43]

A statute of the local community was enacted in 1906. The Jewish Community of Roman consisted of Jews domiciled in Roman and the villages: Elisabeta Doamna, Carol I and Cotu–Vames. The Roman Municipality supervised the administration of the community and controlled it from a financial point of view.

The Community operated the hospital, through the hospital committee, the school, through the school committee and its real estate through the committee of supervision of property: the bathhouse, the warehouse, the houses with adjoining land on Miron Cosatin Street and the land plots in Principatele Unite Street.

In March 1906, the city hall dissolved the existing board, establishing an interim one composed of the following gentlemen: Oisie Vigder, Isac Avram, Iosef Zingher, Zeilig Gelber, Moise Zisman, Leizer Kofler, Simon Hirsch, Iancu Grimberg and Mayer Rothenberg. On 21 January 1907 at the city hall, the election of the Jewish Community Board took place. From 800 voters 210 voted. Declared elected for three year terms with 109 votes were: Iohan Zissu, I. Edelstein, S. Kramer and Noel Bring.[5]

As it was stated in a Jewish newspaper: "In the last few decades, there seems to exist a great deal of apathy and incompetence. The administration founded on the basis of a defective statute, could embezzle funds raised with great sacrifices by members of the community for the building of a school, leaving deficits. This state of affairs lasted until May 1905, when several members called on City Hall, the Mayor being Dr. Riegler, asking for intervention under Article 50 for the organization of urban communities..."

[Page 44]

The 1907–1908 budget reflects that the main income of the Community originated from:

Voluntary payments	lei 38,000
Bath revenues	5,730
School tax/tuition	3,500
Rent income	200
Miscellaneous	3,518
Total	50,948 lei

Expenses rose to 49,207 lei from which:

1 Rabbi, 7 ritual slaughterers)	9,903.60
Administrative personnel	1,290.00
Hospital	9,613.60
Supervision schools	1,650.00

The committee was composed of:

President	M. Stein
Treasurer	Iosub Zingher
Pres. School Committee	M. Zussman
Members	Israel Adelstein W.I. Schwartz Iancu Grunberg[6]

In 1910, the new committee initiated a fundraiser for a new school, and began the construction of new additions to the Jewish school for boys, the hospital, the Home for the Aged and the central bathhouse. All the buildings belonging to the community were appraised at 200,000 lei.[7]

In 1920 the new committee, aware of the lack of funds, decided to rent out the ritual slaughtering of poultry and cattle, hoping to raise approximately 200,000 lei to be used for the upkeep of schools and religious personnel.[8]

Lack of funds was to continue even in 1926, when the committee met to settle the differences between the "Sacra" (the holy) Society and the Community.

[Page 45]

On behalf of the "Sacra" Society participated: Iancu Gros, Bercu Zingher, Mauriciu Rosenberg, and Dr. Ioseph Wacher, and on behalf of the Community Attorney Arnold Cramer, Iulius Istein and Herman Enghelberg. The arbitrators were Attorney Maximilian Schor, Attorney Marcel Zingher, and Suchard Rivenzon. The Community demanded that the "Sacra" Society turn over its surplus funds to the Community, its budget thus becoming an item on the Community budget. The Society's representatives/attorneys felt that this proposal would infringe on its autonomy. The arbitrators reached a compromise: The "Sacra" Society will be administered by a committee composed of two Community members (legal members) and seven members elected by the Society. In the statute of 1926, the characteristics of the prior statute were kept, the sponsorship of the City Hall ceased and the Board of the Community was composed of 21 members divided into four sections: administrative, religious, cultural, welfare, and a committee (section) for the holy sites.

Each section was composed of five wardens, the administrative one of six. All committees constituted the Board of the Community. On 27 February, 1927 the slate advanced by the Community together with the "Sacra" Society was elected.

Administrative Committee: Solomon Joseph, Carol Brand, Moise Abramovici, Moise Sechter, Leon Friedman and Smaie Aizic.

Religious Committee: Iṭic Weisbuch, G. Lazarovici, Leon Goldenberg, Iancu Grunberg and Filip Nadler.

[Page 46]

Welfare: Attorney Saul Herscovici, Haim Smilovici, Simon Moscovici, M. Ehter and Leon Solovici.

Cultural Committee: L. Haimovici, Leon Stein, Ghedale Marcovici, Isac Herscovici and Buium Marcu.[9]

Community elections were also held in the years 1932, 1934, 1936, and 1938. According to the code of the Community of 1936, the Board was to be composed of four sections:

Administrative section: its mission being to maintain and oversee the communal institutions from an administrative point of view, to supervise the execution of the Board budget, exercising constant control over the income and expense and representing the Community in its relationships with other institutions, private or governmental.

Cultural section: its mission was to spread culture and encourage Jewish national sentiments and love of country among the population, and to supervise teaching and education in the boys and girls elementary schools and in the Community nursery schools.

Religious section: was charged with the care for the religious life of the Community, to instill Jewish religious values, to maintain and care for the religious institutions and traditions, and supervise the observation of rituals.

Welfare section: to maintain the hospital and communal bath; to maintain and administer pension funds and aid, and to promulgate the idea of monetary help in the heart of the Jewish population.

[Page 47]

The Community budget was based on the following income sources:

Anonymous contributions
Subsidies from regional and local governments
Revenue from Matzah sales at Passover
Revenue from ritual slaughter of poultry and meat
Income from hospital, schools and baths
Revenue from funeral services and tombstones
Revenues from births and weddings.

In 1936 the Community owned the following institutions: the school for boys with 200 students, the school for girls with 160 students, the kindergarten with 50 children, the hospital providing mostly free services to the Jewish population but also to non Jews, the only bath of the city and the cemetery. It sustained a school dining hall and a home for seniors.[10]

In 1940, with the occasion of Passover, a military canteen was organized where 250 soldiers and displaced Jews were served meals twice a day, lunch and supper.[11]

In June 1941, the permanent commission of the Community Board formed a committee for the resettlement of refugees, composed of: Uşer Beram, Avram Ghertner, Meer Iosub and A. Bayer. Another committee was responsible for the "community work:" Attorney Arnold Cramer, Rabbi Mendel Frankel and B. Friedman. The committee led by Simon Kisler was responsible for the organization and operation of a canteen to feed the needy.

[Page 48]

Delegated with the duty to raise funds for the benefit of evacuees were: Rabbi M. Frankel, Iulius Vigder, Leon Vigder, Leon Grunberg and Lazaar Blecher.[12] Certain publications describe the activities of smaller communities within the former Roman region. In 1932, the Jewish Community of Băceşti-Roman became a judicial entity and its interim Board was composed of Hascal Haimovici – president, S. Sufrin, B. Moscovici, Lazar Kern, B. Grunberg and S. Lazar members. In 1937, the village of Băceşti had a Hebrew school, and a bath maintained by the Community. The president at that time was H. Haimovici and Secretary L. Herscovici.[13]

II: Community Institutions and Concerns

a. Synagogues and the religious personnel

It is believed that a wooden synagogue existed in Roman at the beginning of the 15th century, on the same lot where the Main Synagogue was standing later (in the 20th century). The Great Synagogue was built in 1830 replacing the old synagogue, which burned down in the same year, on the same plot. After its erection, in 1837, the Episcopal Office of Roman sent a petition to Prince Mihail Vodă Sturza, requesting its demolition for being built too close to the Church of St. Nicolae, since the noisy prayers of the Jews were disturbing the tranquility of the Christians in that church. The prince paid no attention to that petition and in 1844 the Episcopal Office sent a new one. Prince Mihail Sturza issued a princely charter, deciding that: "Regarding the number and the location of the synagogues it was clarified that the council considers those synagogues as being deliberately built for the collective worship of the Jews, with the permission of the government. As for the future, the Department shall not allow to build synagogues for the collective worship of the Jews without informing the government and without them being at a distance of about 150 stânjeni [aprox. 150 fathoms or 300 meters, RS] on all sides from the churches". On July 18th, 1844 the „Jewish synagogues" requested the authorization for building a synagogue, without mentioning the distance [from the adjacent church(es), RS]. However, on August 4th, the Prince decides to demolish the synagogues located near churches and to limit the number of synagogues to be erected. To resolve these contradictory decisions, the Prince issues a concluding charter, deciding that the four synagogues in the vicinity of the Church of St. Neculai will remain in their locations for good, and that for the future care should be taken that such things will not occur.

[Page 49]

Now this Great Synagogue remained definitevely on the spot it was erected; in 1952 it was surrounded by a wooden fence. Close to the Moldova river, was standing the „Bait Rishon Bet Hamidrash", founded in 1825 by Sevech Lipscan, a Jew from Roman, member of the „Kasever Chasidim" sect.

A third synagogue, behind the Big Street, was Lipscani (Leipzigher) Synagogue, built in 1835 on the ruins of the dwelling of Rabbi Iancu Beresh. A fourth synagogue was built by Berl Galbeners, in 1852, the fifth was „Bet Hamidrash", founded by Zalman, a sixth was erected in 1865, on the spot of an old synagogue that „belonged to a famous Magid". A seventh synagogue was built by Avram the watchmaker and David Moise, in 1866. The eighth was the synagogue of reb Iosif Galant, behind the Big Street. The ninth was founded by the brothers Kalman Avram and Kalman Nuhem, in 1870. The thenth was that of Rabbi Isacsohn, built in 1865. The eleventh was that of Hersh Beir, built in 1870. The twelveth was of the „Bootmakers", built in the same year. The thirteenth was named „Alt ven Bet Hmidrash", and was built in 1876, near th Big Street [Strada Mare]. The fourteenth was built by Strul Herman in 1881, the fifteenth by Moise Zimand on Sucedava Str. and the sixteenth was the synagogue of Chaim melamed.[14]

[Page 50]

It was proved by tradition that a *heider*, for the instruction of children from the age of six up, was to be found by each synagogue. The Pinkas [register, RS] „Talmud–Tora", found at the „Dr. Iuliu Barasch" Historical Society, proves the existence, in 1817, of a „Talmud–Tora", an instructional institution, more advanced than the *heider*.[15]

In 1910, the synagogue „Bais Sein", on Adrian Str., was built to replace the one ruined.[16]. It will later be named „Spiwak".

From archive documents we learn of the situation of the synagogues and of the religious personnel in 1938.

Synagogue „Rabi Lewi" – founded in 1856 (seems to be the eighth synagogue quoted by S. Wecsler), had 72 worshipers and did not have a statute. The synagogue committee included Solomon Beram and Iosef H. Bentzin. The decisions of the comitee were valid for the members. The property of the synagogue was comprised of: the building, evaluated at 300,000 lei, holy scrolls and religious books, valued at 200,000 lei.

[Page 51]

The budget for the last year (1937) was 50,000 lei. The Rabbi was Israel Friedman, the administrator was Strul Leib Jung, paid 600 lei per month (born in Maramureş).

Synagogue „Michel Leizerovici" – founded in 1878–1880, the initial residence was in the cattle detour way, then in 17 Panaite Donici Str. It had 47 worshipers who were heads of households with a total of aproximately 100 souls. Statutes: the traditional ones.

The council included Iosub Leizerovici, Haim Staermen, Iancu Leizerovici and Iosub Staerman. Its property was comprised of the building, two holy scrolls and 20 old religious books. The budget for the current year was 11,000 lei. The religious personnel included: cantor Iancu Fishel, born in Darabani (Dorohoi), in 1861, and recruited in 1882 in the town of Dorohoi.

Synagogue Feder and Kalman – founded in 1868 (probably the nineth synagogue counted by S. Wecsler), had 100 worshipers. The council included: Sabo Solomon, Carol Nusen, Moise Eisenstein, Isac Farmagiu and Iancu Alter. Its property comprised the building, religious books, candlesticks and three holy scrolls. Its budget for that year was 5,000 lei and it had no religious personnel.

Synagogue „Zalmina" – founded 80 to 90 years back (probably the one founded by Zalman, according to S. Wecsler), had over 200 worshipers and no statute.

Its council members were: Carol Grunberg, S. Aizic, D. Kessler, S. Segal, I. Lustgarten, D. Laufer, A. Isac, David H. Avram and Lupu Schweitzer.

[Page 52]

Its property included the building, valued at 300,000 lei. The budget for the current year was 20,000 lei. The personnel was Rabbi Bercu Schweitzer, who held the certificate of graduation in Jewish studies issued by Rabbi Haim Schor of Bucharest, in 1920, and was a Romanian citizen.

Synagogue „Bait Hadash" – founded in 1860 (probably the sixth of those counted by S. Wecsler), was located at 2 Vlad Țepeș, bought back and transformed in 1880. It had 110 worshipers and a statute of its own voted in 1936. The steering committee was made of: Michel Bruckmayer, Mauriciu Rosenberg, Ghidale Hershcovici, Solomon Vaiser and Moise Schechter.

Its property included the building, furniture, scrolls and the library. The annual budget was 34,028 lei. The religious personnel were cantor Zigmund Wolfsohn, born in Botoșani in 1874, a Romanian citizen and hired by the synagogue in 1904. Quotes from the synagogue statutes:

Article 3 The Scope

The Scope of the Synagogue Society is to maintain the building in clean conditions

To sustain a cantor, a Torah reader (baal–koire) and an attendant (shames).

To conduct a course of specialization in religious prayers for elementary school grade 3 and grade 4 students, during the school holidays.

Article 4. In the event of illness of one of the worshipers, he has to be visited daily...

In case of death at least 10 worshipers will follow the funeral cart to the cemetery and two to three persons will pay a condolence visit.

[Page 53]

Chapter II

Article 8. All worshipers must contribute to the maintenance of the Society with fixed annual contributions.

Synagogue „Bais Iacob" of 10 Vlad Țepeș St.

The statute of Synagogue „Bais Iacov" (of the „Bootmakers") was voted on May 15th, 1938 in the presence of honorables: Samoil Schufer, Moritz Cofler, Marcu Kirerman, Avram Hershcovici, Haim Schwartz, Alter David, Leiba David, Meer Leib, Flitman Ițic Bernfeld, Isac Schor, Marcu Zlociver, presided by Mr. Samoil Schufer. Also present were worshipers Milu Flitman, Sender

Burdujanu, Iosif Schifer, David A. Leiba, Gersen Burdujanu, Moritz Fischer, Buium Marcu, Pincu Kaufman, Soil Marcu, Iosef Goldstein, Hersh Bârlădeanu, and Sender Groper. The content is similar to the one of the previous synagogue.

Rabbi was Meer Isacsohn.

Synagogue „Kol Israel Haverim"

Rabin in 1938 was Froim Weisbuch, born in 1902 and hired in 1927. He complied with the recruitment law, graduated in Theological Studies in 1929.[17]

In old documents the Synagogue „Bait Hadash" is also named „Moshke" and synagogue „Bais Iacov" (of the Bootmakers). On the other hand, new denominations appear, which can hardly be identified: Synagogue Leipzigher is the one mentioned by S.Wecsler as „Lipscanilor", the synagogue founded by Moise Zimand is later called Keiler–Iacob. Synagogues „Kalman Leizer", „Rintzler", „Branishteanu" "Gherşin" and „Spiwak" cannot be identified, at least up to now.[18]

[Page 54]

Synagogues that once existed in the former county of Roman were:

„Tailors'" Synagogue of Tg. (Târgu) Băceşti, founded in 1862, with 70 seats and 32 worshipers (in 1942); Rabbi was Mendel Mark, who also acted as a *shokhet* (kosher slaughterer). He was born in 1890. Zalman Stoleru was caretaker.

Temple „Lapsker" (of the Lipscani) of Tg. Băceşti founded in 1870, with 60 worshipers. The personnel included *shokhet* Leib Stekel and caretaker Iancu Petreanu.

The Great Synagogue of Tg. Băceşti, founded in 1840 with 61 worshipers. Personnel: Avram Aizicovici cantor and David Weintraub caretaker.

The Synagogue in Bozieni – Balş, founded in 1850 with 70 seats and 28 worshipers. Cantor Hune Avram Polak aged 30.

The Synagogue in Dămieneşti, founded in 1850 with 70 seats and 28 worshipers. Personnel: Bercu Bruker rabbi and Itzik Toiv, caretaker. President of the Community was Herşcu Rosenzweig.[19]

The first Rabbi of Roman for whom we possess some information, was David Ber. He was followed by Rabbi Zvi Hersh (or Dov Ber) deceased in 1747;

his son Iehuda Leib deceased in 1745. Other data mentions Rabbi Yitzhak Ben Leib, born in Roman who held office towards the end of the 18th century (1792). The register of the „Ghemilat Chasadim" of 1818 mentions the „Raşkever Rav". In 1823 Rabbi David Ber dies. Between 1825 and 1840 the Rabbinic office was held by Iaakov Berish, named the „Romaner Rav", the forefather of I.B. Brociner. A learned popular orator, he praised the virtues of hand labour.

[Page 55]

In Tzefat he founded a carpet workshop. He traveled to London to resolve a dispute. Between 1839 and 1907 office in Roman was held by Rabbi David Isacsohn, of Reb Premishlaner's family. The Isacsohn family produced many generations of Rabbis; Iacov Isacsohn, Meer Isacsohn, Itzic Isacsohn.

In 1843, Rabbi Isaia Avraham Ben Israel, author of the book *Gheulas Israel* (The Liberation of Israel), died, and in 1857 died Rabbi Froim Iosef Galant. Other documents mention the Tzadik (righteous) David from Roman, the father in law of the Piatra Neamţ Rabbi, Haim Loebel, Rabbi and *shokhet* Segal Coppel, born in 1890 at Tupilaţi – Roman who held office at Bâra – Roman, Rabbi Menahem Mendel of Băceşti, father of Rabbi Yehezkel Mark, also born in Băceşti on January 19th, 1928; he graduated from the Yeshiva "Bet Aharon" from Iaşi and is married to Sara Isacsohn, relative of the Rabbis Isacsohn. The Archives also mention Rabbis Rubin Lipa, Iosub Isacsohn, Solomon Isacsohn and the last Great Rabbi Mendel Frankel, who left a monographic manuscript on the Roman Community.

The documents also mention the *shokhet*s: Schachter Zalman, Leivendman Heindl, Katz Riven, and cantors Kivilevici Marcu, Wolfsohn Zigmund, Strul Leiba.[20]

b. Cemeteries

The Old Cemetery

In the year 1825, the Christian inhabitants of the town, at the direction of the bishop, complained to the prince Ioan Sandu Sturza, demanding the demolition of the cemetery, since it was located "in the middle of the town".

[Page 56]

The prince conducted an investigation, which found the complaint unjustified, and published the following decree in order to finish the conflict:

We, prince Ioan Sturza, by the grace of God, ruler of the country of Moldova.

Following the complaint of the inhabitants of the town of Roman, against the community of the Jews in the town, about the graves that they have for burying the dead, that they are located in the middle of town, and thus annoy gravely the town: questioning the people at the place of the events, we found that the place was used for a long period, from the time the area was not inhabited and not located near a populated area but on a free plot of land; and even now, it is not near the center of the town, but in a suburb far from the town, where it does not disturb anyone. Since the place was used for a long time, and when it was established, it was on free area, we do not find the Jewish community guilty, and we decide that the cemetery will remain in its place, since we don't see that it causes annoyance. On these, this charter is issued by us, the Prince."

1829, the 25th day, number 66.

Despite this decree, the conflict continued. In 1846, following several complaints, the Jewish community of Roman was forced to buy a new place for a cemetery at Râioasa, and close the old one. In 1849, the conflict became even more severe. The mayor Fundăcescu, did not recognize the old cemetery as belonging to the Jews, and commanded to enclose it by a stone fence and plant 200 trees in the area.

[Page 57]

In 1870, a priest, Vasile Brăescu, bought several houses in the neighborhood of the old cemetery, and did not like the cemetery proximity. With the help of his son, Constantin Brăescu, the governor of the Galați County, and the mayor Fundăcescu, they asked the ministry to demolish the cemetery, claiming that cows graze inside it, and also that a tavern is operating, disturbing the peace of the neighborhood.

On 19 Apr 1872, at 3 AM, a group of soldiers and firefighters, led by the mayor Fundăcescu, destroyed the graves, uprooted the trees, and the next day the Jews found the cemetery ruined, and crosses stuck in the place of the graves. The Jews complained to the Ministry of the Interior, who dissolved the city council, and removed Fundăcescu from his job. He became blind and died in misery. On the place of the cemetery they build the "Roman–Vodă" high–school.[21]

In memory of these unfortunate events, an inscription is found in the new cemetery: "On the day of 31 April 1872, against the laws of the Romanian country, paragraph 21 of the Constitution, the Old Jewish Cemetery was destroyed, after almost 300 years of existence."

"The fence, the service buildings and the tombstones were desecrated and shattered, the bones were exhumed, and 2000 trees planted by us, the Israelites, were uprooted. The community has collected 270 sacks of bones and buried them in this cemetery for eternal remembrance".[22]

After the destruction of the cemetery, several funeral inscriptions were published. We read: "The Rabbi from Bozieni, my eyes shed tears for the great eagle with big wings.

[Page 58]

'The dead who were pious are considered alive.' May the soul of Efraim Fişel be bound in the bond of life. May the memory of Efraim Fişel, the son of Israel, deceased on19 Elul (24 Oct 1871) be blessed. May his soul rest in paradise." "In Memory of the Rabbi and preacher, Beer, son of the late Paisech (may his memory be blessed), deceased on 3 Tevet year 5584 (23 Nov 1831)". On the right side of the monument, the following inscription is found: "Merciful Father in Heaven, remember the dead, shed Your light on the soul of the great rabbi Dov Beer the preacher, son of Peisech; shed light on the souls of all our forefathers, whose bones from the old cemetery are buried here; may they rest in peace for eternal remembrance, may their souls raise to paradise. Amen!"[23]

The new cemetery

In 1846 the community has established a new cemetery. Here is the document of purchase of the land:

"The commission for collecting money of the town Roman, for purchasing an estate, in exchange with the holy bishopric:

On 28 July 1846, the leaders of the Jewish nation have paid 45 (forty–five) Lei for a plot of land of 30 *prajini* (a measuring unit of land) with a small house nearby, 223–225 in the Economic Register of 1818, according to the decision of the assembly of the Town Council and affirmed by the Journal of 14 December 1844, the possession of the said site to be reaffirmed once every 20 years.

[Page 59]

To confirm the above, the Signatures:

Secretary Mavrodin, No. 1018

Members Petrovici and Gh. Neculai

The site being insufficient, the community purchased in 1849 another 200 prajini, near the place bought in 1846, with the condition of paying for the leasing 20 years in advance. These two places make up the new cemetery. The purchase act is as following:

"The committee for collecting money of the town Roman, for purchasing an estate, in agreement with the holy bishopric, 29 May 1949:

The sum of 600 [six hundred) Lei was paid by the Jewish community of this town, for 200 *prăjinni,* for the burial of their deceased, located in the periphery of the town in the rural area, in accordance with the decision of the Municipal Assembly on 14 December 1844 about the lease of the site, to be reviewed every 20 years.

Confirmed by the signatures of the members and the seal of the Committee:"

Signed: Gedeon Erromonach, Ion Petrovici Caminar, Ion Neamtu Postelnic.[24]

The *Pinkas* (Register) of the "Hevra Kadisha" [Jewish Burial Society] of Roman (1794)

In the old times the offices of the "Hevra Kadisha" [Burial Society, lit. "sacred society"] were situated on the premises of the community, which managed not only the cemetery, but also other community institutions, and collected taxes as well. The community was taking care of the public bath-house, the poor, the widows, the orphans and the sick.

The register thus contains also the rights and duties of the members of the congregation. The introduction contains also moral concepts.

[Page 60]

The *Pinkas* records the changes in the religious personnel, leaders, service people, *şamaşim* [synagogue attendants]. Among the first signatures we note: Meir David of Roman, Hilel Meir of Roman, Haim son of Haim of Roman. The addition "of Roman" emphasizes that those people were born in the town, as we continue to read signatures without such an addition, Moşe son of David, Tivi son of the late Iţhak, David Aharon son of şelomo.

Some of the people's names are prefixed by the title Rabbi. This title is used as an honorific, and does not mean that the person was a Rabbi.

In the 19th century, people adopted family names. We find signatures of Haim Moshe Katz, Zeev Wolf Davidovitz, Aizic ben David Zilberman. Some names are of Russian origin, some of Austrian. The service people have signed their names following the importance of their job: şelomo Iehuda, şameş gadol (chief attendant). On page 25 we find the following inscription, written in print letters: "For remembrance, that the members of the "Sacra" Society have committed themselves before the famous and enlightened Rabbi of Iaşi, the capital, to donate to the "Hevra Kadisha" each year two tallers."

The "Hevra Kadisha" was founded in Roman, in 1794. From the notes in the register we believe that it was founded even before. The first notes do not follow any chronological order. The first one is from 1784, the second from 1785, the third from 1786, but the fourth is from 1774, followed by 1775, 1782, 1784, etc.

[Page 61]

In the register, we find a note in Hebrew, from 1867, about the attempt of the mayor Mihai Fundăcescu, to destroy the cemetery – unsuccessful then, but realized in 1872. At that time the mausoleum above the Rabbi's grave was destroyed, as well as the hut where the guard Avraham Chetraru has lived (probably chetraru was his occupation – stoneworker). The community, led by Rabbi David Iţhak, hired people to exhume the bodies, filling up 300 sacks, and burying them in the new cemetery.

Until the 80s of the 19th century, the notes in the Register used only Hebrew. From 1880, non–Hebrew expressions appear. The dates are not noted using the Jewish calendar any more. A mixture of Hebrew and Romanian is frequently used as in "The President Mr. Katz proposed to resign" (some of the words in Hebrew, others in Romanian).[25] In 1889, the Jewish leader Aba Abram, sold the Register to the Historical Society "Iuliu Barasch."[26]

c. The Bathhouse. Insuring the Kosher Food Supply

The bathhouse existed since the beginning of the XIX century; in 1835 it was destroyed. In 1865, the City Hall asked the Community to repair the bathhouse and install drainage. In 1892, the Community Committee purchased for the local Jewish needs a bath (building and infrastructure) worth 95,000.00 lei. This purchase was accomplished through special contributions and efforts of Meer Heller and David Lustgarten, the President of the community, and the Secretary Isidor Schimschen.[27]

[Page 62]

The bathhouse was modernized in 1912; it was located in the center of the Jewish settlement in Roman. In the courtyard it had three tanks of 15 meters deep. These tanks were supplying the ritual baths with natural fountain water. The bathouse was fitted with bath tubs, 1st and 2nd class, with two ritual pools and a steam bath.[28]

In 1924, the Jews of Bozieni requested an authorization for the construction of an organized bath, from their own resources.[29]

The Community Board built on the site of the central bath a warehouse for *matzot* [special Passover bread]. The profit therefrom was to be donated to the poor. M. Silberman donated a machine to fabricate the *matzot*.

d. Social welfare and health

Charity was practiced by Jews for a long time and in various forms, individually or on an organized level, to help other Jews as well as non Jews. In 1844, two Jews from Roman, Iţic Nadler and Avram Faibiş donated the sums of 700 and 600 lei respectively for the fire victims from Huşi and Iaşi.[31]

Between the years 1862–1864, Luca Moise, a shoemaker born in Roman, bequeathed his property to the hospital, school and Jewish community from Ploeşti. In this period, Dr. David Reitman donated a certain amount of money to the Home for the aged "Elena Doamna."[32]

In 1877, the pharmacist from Roman, Max Frankel made a donation to the Roman school.[33] In 1887 and 1906 respectively, the Roman Jews donated various sums of money to the fire victims of Roman and Botoşani.[34] Philanthropy appears in Roman in an organized form in 1812, in the form of the *Bikkur Cholim Society* (helping the sick, lit. visiting the sick).

[Page 63]

Also mentioned is the Society of Welfare *Ghemilath Hasadim* [loan–without–interest fund].[35] On the site of the old *hekdeş* [poor house] in 1900 they founded the Home for the Aged, subsidized during the inter–war years by the local authorities. It is mentioned in the Romanian Encyclopedia, vol. II, 1938.[36]

In the same year, a communal kitchen for feeding the poor was established and in 1941 a canteen for everyone.[37]

Each edition of by–laws of the Community provided for these duties; in the last two, from 1926 and 1935, there are special provisions for social assistance. Between 1941 and 1944, these became very important, due to the general poverty of the Jewish population.

Although with certain exceptions, Jews were received without difficulty in public hospitals, but due to the lack of kosher food, they built their own. The Jewish hospital of Roman dates back to 1811.[38] Before that there was an institution that hosted poor Jews in transit, where medical services were also provided. It was located near the old cemetery and was still in existence in 1870.[39] In 1836 the hospital was functioning, marked as lot number 513 on the map of the town of Roman. The building was located between the Jewish schools and the bathhouse. In 1853, with the occasion of taking by the community the exclusive right to bake "bread and pretzels," the hospital is again mentioned; from the net income, the Community hoped to be able to build new buildings for the bath and hospital, the existent ones being "totally dilapidated".

[Page 64]

Unable to build a memorable new hospital at that time, on the front of the bathhouse a slab with the following inscription was mounted: "Our voice is loud among the Jews: take note and be forewarned that our decision will never change, because the majority of the congregants of the town voted and confirmed, under the weight of their oath and threat of excommunication, that the income from the bath will serve exclusively for the maintenance of the sick in the hospital and will not be changed for ever!" Year 1856.[40] The new hospital was established in 1879, near the communal bath, led by Dr. Eliad and the pharmacist Max Frenkel, having 10 beds.[41] The Community also began to maintain the sick in their own homes. In 1879, poor sick who could not be accommodated in the hospital, stayed home where they were visited by a physician and received medications gratis furnished by the pharmacist Max Frenkel, with a 25% discount on taxes. In 1882, the hospital was renovated and the furnishings improved. They raised the roof and built a balcony with windows, and the entire building became more prominent in appearance.[42] The first physician employed by the hospital was Dr. Adolf Elias. On 25 July 1885, the Community designated a committee charged with the hospital administration, to renovate and refurbish. The committee consisted of: Moise Schiffer, Isac Avram and Abram Mark, The hospital had six beds for men, and four for women. It was led by Dr. Leo Robener who would later be decorated by the emperor of Austria with the Order "Franz Josef", and the title of cavalier.[43] The Jewish hospital, the committee's president being Max Schiffer, "progressed steadily, from the ruins that it was, to become a pleasant home for the sick, well furnished, new beds, with two covers, one for summer, one for winter, and two pillows each."[44]

[Page 65]

In the old hospital, the sick were attended, from 1816, by two medics, Anbele and Samoil, whose homes bordered the hospital. After 1853, they were joined by the surgeon, David Reitman, with a degree from Pesta dated 1840. In 1864 he became doctor at the Precista Hospital in town, since 1866 a private doctor in Roman and between 1850 and 1857 a physician in the Jewish Hospital.[46] Another doctor in the Jewish Hospital was Dr. Morris Frei, deceased in 1882.

A physician whom I mentioned already was Dr. Leo Rabener, who came from Vienna in 1885. He was a learned man, a good practitioner, knowledgeable in ophthalmology and dentistry. He elevated the prestige of the institution, which made significant advancements. Due to lack of physicians in the county, he was recruited to work as a regional doctor, assigned in 1891 to the Siretul de Sus region, with residence in Bâra, then to Plăşile Unite [United Regions] with residence at Dulceşti. In 1912, after helping inaugurate the new building, he left the town and settled in Cernăuţi. Rabener was followed by Dr. Leon Henic, a distinguished figure of the Roman medical profession, then Max Ghinsberg. Also employed were assistant surgeons Avram Ghelber, and in 1904 Iancu Lazarovici.[47]

The Roman Jews were treated, in the hospital or clinic, also by Dr. Scrob, of whom, however, there were complaints.[48] In 1885, M. Gross, a dentist from Galaţi, settled in Roman, on Stefan the Great Street, in Mr. Roiu's houses.

[Page 66]

In his dental clinic one could have "dentures sustained only through air pressure, according to the most modern techniques".[49] Dr. V. Gomoiu also mentions the dentist Josef Loefler, at the end of the previous century.[50] In 1880 and 1892, the hospital had 10 beds, in 1908 – 12 beds.[51] In 1933 the upkeep of the hospital cost the community 169,000.00 lei annually. The hospital was directed by Dr. A. Wechsler and Dr. T. Wachtel and provided care to 5,500 citizens annually; 178 of them were hospitalized. The hospital also provided free medicines.[52] In 1941, 10 rooms of the hospital were taken over by the authorities, 4 rooms left with almost non existent activity. During the war, Jewish doctors who had remained in Roman organized for the Jewish sick a hospital in the houses of the Negruzi Palace. It was named "Spitalul Orăşenesc," [the town hospital], in reality being a mere quarantine, poorly maintained due to the well known shortages. It was managed by Dr. Benţin Hascal, helped by a group of doctors and pharmacists.[53]

After the war, the Jewish Hospital had to be reorganized and refurbished, having been disowned of all of medical instruments and furnishings. Dr. B. Leizer and Attorney Bayer went to Bucharest to intervene with the well-connected Ţipra Lupu in the name of the town community.[54]

Covering the period 1942–1944, the lists show 24 doctors, 4 dentists and 19 dental assistants. One more word to remember those who were deported to Transnistria: Dr. Bozianu Iosub, Dr. Dulberger Marcel, Dr. Ghertner Iancu and Dr. Iosepovici Maer (Secretary General of the Jewish Community from Savrani–Balta Colony).

[Page 67]

In 1940, Dr. Rămureanu Aurel who functioned in Strunga–Roman was also available and was recruited to the detachment of m.o. Floreşti.[55]

After the war, the Precisa Hospital was reopened and attending were among others, Dr. Benţin Hascal, Dr. Cahane Leizer, Dr. Velt Levi, and Dr. Dulberger Marcel.[56] As a point of information, we mention the interest of some Jewish medical students in Romanian popular medicine in the former Roman county: Juster A. Jean (Pănceşti– Roman), Mintzer Bercu, Mantel Hirsch, Berman Iosif, Leon Sachs, Hirsch M., Smilovici Zalman, Burăch Avram, Mathias Avram, Wisner Leon.[57] Dr. Mauriciu Blumenthal (1895–1955) was born in Roman, later to become member of the faculty at the Dermatology Clinic of Bucharest.[58]

At the beginning of the XIX century, there were in Roman shopkeepers of "poisonous substances" (medical drugs), such as Mr. Strul from the stories of the writer Ion Creangă; in 1832, are mentioned Herşcu, in 1838, the Jew Baroh son of Calman, dealer in medicinal drugs. In 1852 "an inspection of the poisonous drugs held by Solomon Rentler found them to be in order."[59]

A controversial figure was Iosef Bredmeier, originally from Germany, so that in fact his correct name would be Wredemayer. He worked between 1844 and 1845 in Galaţi; in 1846 he worked in Roman and between 1850 and 1855 in Tîrgul Neamt; he had a degree from the University of Vienna and according to the archives he was Jewish.[60]

[Page 68]

Since 1876, in Roman operated the pharmacist Max Fankel, born in Iaşi in 1845, married Babette (born 1858); their son Alexandru was born in Roman in 1879. Max Frankel graduated from the faculty of pharmacy at the University Ludwig–Maximilian in Munich, in 1874.[61]

In 1879, his lease on the pharmacy was extended for a five year term, on the following conditions:

To complete the improvements of the pharmacy laboratory, so that it will serve both pharmaceutical as well as chemical objectives.

To complete the improvements of the storage room with the necessary provisions and to improve the basement, which served as a warehouse.

For the term of the lease, to make available free medication to the hospital employees.[62] In 1872, the pharmacist Leon Rozici operated in Băceşti[63]

Among the graduates of the pharmacy faculty of the University of Munich, was I. Reitman, the son of the Roman doctor.[64]

During WWI there functioned in Roman the Military Hospital No. 242, where working as a pharmacist's aide was H. Coniver, the medical student and brother of the pharmacist Lupu Coniver. The student was handing out basic medicines and band aids, from the stock. Surgeon's assistant Iancu Velt, researchers Aaron Stangel and Bubi Schmautz also worked in this hospital, since the physicians Leon Henic and Max Ginsberg were recruited to the army.[65]

[Page 69]

In the appendices we find the names of 15 Jewish pharmacists of Roman, working between 1942 and 1944. Among them we note Flexer Lipa and Brucmaer Zalman, who graduated from the Biochemistry Faculty and Weintraub Ozias, doctor in pharmacy sciences from the University of Turin.

We have certain information about the pharmacist Iosepovici Şloim, graduate of the University of Pharmaceutical Sciences in Bucharest in 1928. He was born in Roman in 1902, his father Moise Iosepovici, was a carriage painter. He completed the elementary school and high school in his native city. His brother, Dr. Maer Iosipovici, was deported to Transnistria, he maintained connection with him through a variety of clandestine couriers, through whom he would send to the detainees clothing, food and money, risking his own life.

Dr. Pharmacist Vasile Lipan offers us information about other pharmacists in town: Horovitz Iosef, graduate of the Pharmacy Faculty at the Iaşi University. In 1927 he bought the "Minerva" pharmacy. Rabinovici Ghizela (born 1888) obtained the pharmacy concession at Bozieni, etc.[66]

e. Jewish Schools in Roman

The educational system of the Romanian Jews consisted of the *Bet–Hamidrash* and the *heider*. There used to be many *hadarim* in Roman; from about 1870 to about 1880 there were more than 20, of which some continued to exist up to the present days, when both the Community Jewish School and the attendance of Jewish children at state schools blew a finishing stroke to the *heider*, so beautifully brought up by Bialik.

[Page 70]

By the third decade of the 20ᵗʰ century, about four *hadarim* still functioned in the city, of which that of the elderly Bloch and the one of Mrs. Rivenzon can be mentioned.

A higher school than the *heider*, the *Talmud Tora*, existed in Roman which, situated on the bank of the Moldova River was supposed to be in existence for about three centuries, namely founded in about 1680.

That situation continued up to 1859, when Minister Cantacuzino summoned the Roman Community leaders to Iaşi, inviting them to found a modern Jewish School in Roman. The Community President, Aba Abram, tried to establish the school, but failed and the *Talmud–Tora* continued to exist until 1868, headed by Adolf Gross, with three teachers for Romanian, Hebrew and German. The Mayor of Roman, V. Agarici, insisted in 1865 on building a synagogue and a modern school; as long as he served as mayor he had the best sentiments for Jews (sentiments inherited by his descendant Mrs. Viorica Agarici).[67] The Town Hall insisted and in 1866 proposed a lot for the school building. On November 17th 1866, the Community, represented by Avram Cramer, Aba Abram and Itic ben Marcu, acquired from Vasile Makarovici and David Litenschi the inn and the lot with the cellar, named „Hanul Mungiului", for the price of 750 gold coins, with a down payment of 120 gold coins, the rest to be payed in further installments.

The school began to function in 1867, headed by Alfred Ravici, with a teaching staff composed of: Zeilig Şor, Defin, Israel Moise Steinholtz, Samuel Lam, Moise Landman and Vulcu Cucu.

[Page 71]

Yet, in 1872, the lawyer Gh. Hotineanu, son in law and proxy for Vasile Maharovici, filed a motion for annulling the contract for the purchase of „Hanul Mangiului" on the pretext that the remaining installments for the purchase were not made in time. In 1873, the court decided that... „Considering that of the parties to the contract, the buyers are of Jewish nationality... the presented document is declared null and void by law". A complete restitution was ordered, without taking into account the money already paid by the Jews; to that day the Community had already paid 555 gold coins. The Jews addressed the Justice Ministry and the US consul, B. Peixoto, but to no avail.

In 1879, a committee composed of Haim Gălă?anu, Manase Zilberman, Pincu ben Leiba and DR. D. Lustgarten began the struggle again. They bought, in 1880, for 280 gold coins, the houses and the lot on Mohoreni St. and located the *Talmud–Tora* there. The school had a teaching staff composed of Moses Schwartz, Volf Mantel, Itic Orenstein. The curriculum was close to that of the state primary education, but the study of Hebrew was given priority. In 1893, by the amendment to the education law introduced by A. C. Cuza and supported by A. Delimarcu, the deputy from Roman, the Jewish children were excluded from the state primary schools. As of November 1st, 1893, a primary superior school, named „The Israelite–Romanian School" and supported by the Community was founded in Roman.[68] N. Bellu was appointed principal. At the inauguration, speeches were made by I. Schimshen, on behalf of the local community committee, by principal N. Bellu, Dr. Miron and I. Catz.

[Page 72]

They stressed the importance of the institution. Donations were made for the poor students of the school.

The school had three classes with eight teachers: three teachers of the Romanian language, two teachers of the German language and three who taught Talmud.[69] Prof. A. S. Rapaport published, in Hebrew, an account of the first five years of school activity. The teachers hired for teaching Hebrew were: A. S. Rapaport, professor and publicist, the mentor of many generations of Jewish children, I. Moscovici, M. Valter, I. Orenstein, M. Schwartz and S. Feier, and those hired for teching Romanian were: M. Rămureanu and Bejenaru.

In the following year, the committee, with the help of the president of the Community, hired I. Goldenthal as principal, but as the laws permitted only a Christian principal, they hired, in 1896, Grădinaru E. for that position. He officiated as principal till 1899. By hiring him, the definitive authorization for the school was obtained in October 1896.

In the same year, Avram Suchar was hired as Hebrew teacher. At the end of the 19th century, the school was divided into two sections: one with 4 classes in the Mavrichi house on Tipografiei St. and the other with the same number of classes in the Holtzman house. In 1898, thanks to the efforts of M. Stein, the school moved to the old Post Office building, which later housed the girls' school, the kindergarten and the school's canteen. Under the direction of Naum Paraschiv (1899–1908) the following have taught the Romanian language subjects, each for two years: Carp, Friedman, Zagar, Fruchtman, Aroneanu, Crighel and Rosner. A special element was the teacher A. S. Segal, who relocated from the school in Roman to the sefardi school in Bucharest.

[Page 73]

With the help of the committee, following Astruc's visit, and with the assistance of enlightened and decisive figures as Dr. Henic and Iancu Gross, the teachers' two–months vacation was introduced. The number of the children [attending the school, RS] increased to 225 in 1904 and to 270 pupils in 1905.[70]

The girls' school and the fourth grade opened for the school year of 1901–1902. Ms. Leibovici and Ms. Ackerman continued to hold the directing positions.[71]

According to the I.C.A. report for 1903, regarding the situation of the schools in Romania, functioning in Roman were:

The boys's school with 4 grades and 294 registered pupils, 120 in grade I, 77 in grade II, 70 in grade III and 27 in grade IV. Teaching were four instructors of the Romanian language and five teachers of the Hebrew language.

The girl's school with 249 pupils in the four grades, as follows: in grade I – 119, in grade II – 58, in grade III – 51 and in grade IV – 21. The teaching staff included four lady teachers and two teachers of the Hebrew language.

It is mentioned that I.C.A. renewed the relations with the Schooling Board of Roman and handed over the subsidy for the first semester of the school year 1902–1903.[72]

In the school year 1907–1908, the boys' school had 226 pupils, while the girls' school had 179 pupils. During the period of December 1st 1907 to March 31st 1908, the community allocated the sum of 16,293 lei to the schools.[73]

In 1879, when the *Talmud–Tora* was reorganized, an institution which distributed food and clothing to the poor children was founded. During 25 years it functioned as a private initiative. In 1903, the foundations for the „School Canteen" Society were laid, its first steering committee being composed of: Simon Mark, Noel Bring, Nathan Bandel, Z. Baier, Michel Șapira and Itic Mark. This committee also established the definitive rules for helping the poor pupils. The first funds were obtained from the donations of Baron Hirsch, a French Jewish philanthropist.

[Page 74]

The balance sheet of this society for the period of October 1st, 1904 to July 1st, 1905 shows that food was provided for 63 boys and 20 girls, pupils of the Community Schools. During 115 days, 9,409 portions of food were served. In addition, clothing was supplied to all pupils. In 1907, the society collected 935 lei through donation lists, with which it clothed 50 boys and 20 girls, pupils of the Hebrew schools. It also received, as in other years, a donation of a measure of wood and 10 lei from Mrs. Maria L. Bogdan–Gădin?i. In the following years the „School Canteen," presided by Mr. Iosef Neulicht, also distributed clothes and boots to the poor pupils.

After WWI, the „School Canteen" had a suitable location in the girls' school building, with a fully furnished mess hall, a complete set of kitchenware and a daily supply of two dishes of hot food to the children. At the beginning of each school year, 40 of them were dressed with coats and fur caps. The poor children were also offered free books and writing materials and at the deserving among them were given awards at the end of the year.[74]

On June 21st 1909, the foundation stone for the new building of the local Hebrew school was laid. To the raising of funds contributed: Iancu Avram, A. Kalmanowitz, Noel Bring, M. Zissman, Iancu Grunberg, M. Frost, Iosef Weiss, Moise Stein and Avram Laver.

[Page 75]

A large public participated in the ceremony of laying the foundation stone, including the County Prefect, A. Delimarcu.[75]

This was the text of the inscription:

"With the help of God,

The Israelite Community of Roman has built with its own means, during the years 1909–1910, the Hebrew–Romanian Primary School for Boys, founded in 1868. The construction took place during the glorious reign of Their Royal Majesties, King Carol I and Queen Elisabeta, heirs to the thone being Their Royal Highnesses, Prince Ferdinand and Princess Maria. The construction committee was composed of the gentlemen Iancu Avram, Moise Forst, Iosef Weiss, Avram Laver, Moise Stein, Altăr Calmaovici, Noel Bring, Moise Zusman and Iancu Grunberg, which collected the donations specified below:

The present trusteeship of the Israelite Community, presided by Moise Stein, from budgetary income, 21,150 lei.

The Israelite (Jewish) Community members, specified in „The Golden Book" and in the accounts rendered, in the years 1909–1910 contributed 5,939 lei.

The trusteeship of the Israelite Community of the year 1904, presided by Iosef Weiss – 1,500 lei

The „Sacra" Society – 3,000 lei

The School Committee presided by Noel Bring and Isidor Schiffer, from festivities, for furniture – 2,100 lei.

Mrs. Fani and Moise Forst – 1,200 lei

Mrs. Elise and Mr. Iancu Spodheim – 1,200 lei

[Page 76]

Mrs. Netti and Mr. Richard Stoorfer – 1,000 lei

Mrs. Paulina and Mr. Ch. Şmilovici – 1,010 lei

The „Progresul" lodge XII.393 I.O.B.B., president Iancu Avram, from festivities 917 lei

Mrs. Adela and Mr. Avram Laveri – lei 800

Mrs. Clara and Mr. Iancu Avram – lei 625

Miss Henele and Mr. Milu Sommer – 625 lei

D. M. Stâncă (pharmacist) – 500 lei

Mrs. Rachel and Mr. Oişie Vigder – 500 lei

Mrs. Rachel and Isidor Bring – 500 lei

Mrs. Roşca and Mr. Avram Moses – 500 lei

Mrs. Rebeca and Mr. Israel Adelstein – 500 lei

The Roman Sugar Factory – 510 lei

The School Canteen, presided by Mr. I. Neulicht, from festivities – 500 lei

The building entrepreneur was Mr. M. Bruckmaier."

The memorial document was signed by the school building committee and by all those present. The great fighter for Jewish causes, Iancu Avram, former president of the I.O.B.B. „Progresul" lodge, delivered a speech. Telegrams of homage were sent to King Carol I and to the Ministry of Public Education. Here is their response:

"From the bottom of my heart I wish that this school will become a true center of the Romanian culture and feelings. Your deeds and the devotion you showed to the fulfillment of the task you took upon yourselves, deserves all the praise from righteous men and from all those who think and feel Romanian" (Minister V. Gh. Mortun).

[Page 77]

The works conducted by entrepreneur Michel Bruckmaier made fast advance, so that in October 1910 the school opened with new furniture and new didactic material, with a turnout of 226 pupils, under the management of Iosef Neulicht. The building became the property of the Community in 1908, later becoming the venue of the girls' school. Between 1909 and 1916 the following functioned here: Fany Schapira, Bandel, M. Hainsohn, Wechselberg, Leibovici, Lazăr Rapaport, Iosef Neulicht, Frederica Wagschel, and for the Hebrew language, after the teacher Avram Suchăr left for Bucharest, Lozner, I. Naiman, Moses Schwartz, Samuel Lamm and Fişel Boch. The activity of teacher Ruca Axelrad must be especially mentioned. The continuity was assured for the Hebrew language by the late Rapaport and for the Romanian language by Suchard Rivenzon, hired in 1908, who served one year at the „Cultura" school in Iaşi, after his graduation from the Teachers' Training School in Paris.[76] After the mobilization [for WWI, RS] was declared, the school was evacuated and fitted out as a hospital and the children were relocated to synagogues, where classes were organized, under the guidance of A. S. Rapaport and I. Naiman. After the war, the school reopened, having S. Rivenzon as principal with the teaching staff composed of Iancu Reiza, Tudic for the Romanian language and also Rapaport, I. Naiman, Fişel Boch and Moses Schwartz. Later teaching Romanian were: P. Cocea, C. Muraru, C. Pippă, Gh. Ghiorghiasa, Ernani Cristea, Gh. Uscatu and V. Mancaş. In the school committees of the post–war period the following took part: Iancu Gross, Arthur Schor, then the gentlemen Avram Laver, Itic Grunberg, Isak Mark who presided up to 1921, then Heinrich Haimovici and Moisă Rosenberg.

[Page 78]

In 1920, the documents in the archive mention the existence of the following Jewish schools in Roman: The Hebrew–Romanian School for Boys, The Hebrew–Romanian School for Girls and The Hebrew–Romanian Commercial School.[77]

Some of the city's notable intellectuals were members of the school committees: Lawyer Maximilian Schor, Att. Arnold Cramer, Dr. M. Helfont, Dr. M. Ghinsberg, Dr. I. Wacher and Pharmacist I. Horowitz.

In September 1924, the Moldova Jewish Teaching Staff held its meeting in Roman. The committee was reconstituted: President – Suchard Rivenzon, Secretary A. Band – school inspector. The new primary education law regarding the Jewish teaching staff was debated.[78]

From 1925 on the following also participated in the school committees: H. Gelber, Leopold Haimovici, the teacher N. Konig, Carol Grunberg, Dr. Iosef, Lupu Schmeltzer, Att. I. Schwartz, Pincu Caufman and H. Grunberg.

In 1927 the permission to advertise was granted to the Hebrew–Romanian School. It was the first Jewish school in Moldova to receive that permission.[79]

Donations and Legacies

Mr. Adolf and Dr. Iosef Wacher: 150 educational pictorials.

A. Rosenberg Family: the Hebrew library and 20 educational pictorials.

Mrs. and Mr. Pharmacist I. Horowitz, Mrs. and Mr. Rubin Chitzman, Mr. B. Brucăr and Smaie Aizic Bercovici – various materials and prizes.

[Page 79]

Donation Mauriciu Blanc – Bucharest – 1921

Legacy of Rosa Schönberg – New York – 20,000 grants (prize for the best Hebrew Language scholar)

Legacy „Rebeca and Azril Adelstein" offered by „Bercu and Sofia Zingher from whose income prizes valuing 500 lei (annually) were granted

Legacy „Betty and Moritz Wachtel" – an annual prize of 500 lei.

A prize offered annually by lawyer Dr. M. Zingher, for endowing a graduate to learn a trade.

The contribution of the „Small Credit Bank", which gave a sum for rewarding industrious pupils.

Teaching Staff for the year 1932–1933

S. Rivenzon, permanently appointed teacher and principal, with a tenure of 25 years in the education field.

Iosef Naiman, permanently appointed teacher, with an experience of 20 years.

Elias Feldstein, temporary teacher with a yearly appointment, working for 12 years.

Gh. Uscatu, state appointed teacher, working for 11 years.

Vasile Mancaş, teacher.

Dr. Fany Horowitz, temporary teacher.

Gherş Moldovanu, temporary teacher.

The following were inspectors at the schools: C. Dafinescu, Nae Ionescu, Simionescu, P. Gheorghiasa, and V. Rollea (in the years 1893–1933). Extracted from the reports: "The maintenance of the building shows the principal is working hard to raise the standards of the school to the level it deserves" (Aron Barid) and "The pupils of the school have a thorough preparation due to the auxiliary staff, that completes, increases and clarifies the facts that were taught. The library of the school was founded by Mr. Rivenzon" (P. Gheorghiasa).

[Page 80]

Suchard Rivenzon: A former pupil of the Jewish–Romanian school in Roman (1896–1900), teacher from the year 1909, and principal from 1916. His extra–curricular activity includes: the author of the work "What is education", prized by the association of the higher education graduates "Unirea," speaker at various cultural associations, collaborator at newspapers, as well as professional and general periodicals. Member of various cultural and philanthropic associations, past senator. Was awarded distinctions:

"Multumiri Ministeriale" (Ministerial Thanks – 1929), "Avbntul Ţării" (Country Enthusiasm – 1913), "Crucea Comemorativă" (Commemorative Cross – 1916–1918), "Victoria–1918" (Victory), "Coroana Rombniei" (Romanian Crown – 1922).

The book by S. Rivenzon, that I have consulted, was part of the Rosenberg Library, then belonged to the pharmacist I. Caufman – Roman, then to dr. E. Cozărăscu.

Iosef Neuman, (remark by Dr. E. Cozărăscu) – teacher at the Israelite-Romanian school in Roman, died on 7 Nov 1944, hit by a military car. Taken to the local hospital, has passed away after several hours.

In 1933, the boys' school had 211 pupils (Principal S. Rivenzon), and the girls' one had 136 pupils (Principal Clara Segal). For each of those schools, the community has spent 235000 lei that year.

[Page 81]

Following is a list of Hebrew manuals that belonged to the school:

Laşon Hazahav, 1910, Edition Samitca, Craiova, author S. Gold.

Micra Codeş, 1904.

Sefer hatefila (book of prayers), 1900

The elements of the Hebrew language, 1909

Pentateuch, 1903

The kindergarten functioned since 1928, received operation permit in 1930. Until 1937 it was supervised by A.C.F.E. (the Cultural Association of Jewish Women) and after that by the community. At this institution have worked: Tony Avram, Raşela Rivensohn. The board of the kindergarten included: the lawyer I. Schwartz, Miss. S. Şmilovici, Herman Marcu and Carolina Goldenberg.

In 1940, the boys' school was requisitioned, and the studies continued in the girls' school. All Jewish teachers and pupils have been expelled from the Romanian schools. For example, we shall mention the teachers Abraham Hollingher and Iacob Konig.

In Roman, in the years 1940 – 1944, two elementary schools operated (one for boys, one for girls), 1–2 high schools, and a kindergarten.

1940 – 4 schools; one kindergarten, two elementary schools, one high school, teaching staff 27, pupils 582, kindergarten 50, elementary 440, high school 92.

1941 – 4 schools; teaching staff 42, pupils 627, kindergarten 55, elementary 435 (161 girls), high school 137.

[Page 82]

1942– Five schools; one kindergarten, two elementary, two high schools, teaching staff 44, pupils 690, kindergarten 55, elementary 470, high school 160.

1943– Five schools as above, pupils 659, kindergarten 50, elementary 440, high school 165.

In October 1942, the schools were based in the following locations:

The girls' elementary school, the site of the school at no. 3 Miron Costin Street.

The boys' elementary school, at the synagogues Croitori (Tailors), Centrala, Moşke, Spivack.

The Jewish high school, at the site in no. 79 Sucedava Street.

The kindergarten, at the same site.

Additional parallel classes were opened, for I, II and III grades, when the number of pupils in a class passed 55.

The teaching staff:

At the boys' school:

Mr. Camille Beer, principal and teacher of Romanian Language (in the year 1941/1942, Meer Iosub, bachelor of law, served in this position)

Miss. Schwartz Margareta, high school graduate in 1932, teacher of Romanian Language.

Dr. Jeny Şaim, bachelor in literature, teacher of Romanian Language.

Dr. Bella Iohan, high school graduate, teacher of Romanian Language.

Sabo Salomon, teacher of Hebrew Language and religion, graduated from the Rabbinic Seminar in 1933.

Additional teachers were Ilie Leizer, Ţalic Leon, and Iosefina Marcus.

[Page 83]

Girls' school:

Fany Horowitz, principal and teacher of Romanian Language, bachelor of literatures and philosophy, Iasi University, 1932.

Rebeca Pincu, high school graduate, teacher of Romanian Language.

Roza Steinberg, teacher of Romanian Language, graduate of the Academy of Commercial Studies.

Hermina Hirsch, teacher of Romanian Language.

Gherş Moldoveanu, born at Băl–i in 1897, graduate of the Private Seminar in Lida, Lithuania, worked in 1930–1939 in the boys' school, and from 1939 in the girls' school.

Isacsohn I–ic David, Rabbi, graduate of the "Beit– Israel" secondary rabbinic school in Buhuşi, licensed by the ministry of religion and public instruction 1909.

Additional teachers of the Hebrew Language:

Josef Naiman (Neuman), born in Botoşani in 1880, graduate of the Sambur–Gali–ia Yeshiva, in 1902. Passed the exams in Romanian Language and was hired in 1913 as teacher of Hebrew and religion.

Moses Mendel, teacher of Hebrew language and Jewish religion, graduate of the Hebrew pedagogic seminar in Satu–Mare, passed the exams in Romanian language.

Solomon Sabo, graduate of the Hebrew and Rabbinic seminar at Vişeul de sus, Maramureş; had the right to publish; passed the exams of the Romanian language and was hired in 1925.

[Page 84]

Iancu Horodniceanu, graduate of 6 high–school classes, teacher.

The mixed theoretic high–school:

Avram Iacob, licentiate in literature and philosophy, taught Latin and Greek.

Volfsohn Munisch, graduate of the faculty of literature and philosophy, taught history.

Eng. Beer Camille taught a complementary course.

Baer Aizic, Ph.D. in Romanian Law, taught Romanian Language.

Segal Iosub, licentiate in Law, taught Latin.

Racz. Vasile, M.D., Paris, taught French.

Solomon Nahuma, (after marriage Maxim, deceased in 1989), licentiate in letters, taught German.

Iancu Marcel, licentiate in law, taught geography.

Weidenfeld Fany, licentiate in mathematics, taught mathematics.

Curelaru Gherşin, student of mathematics, taught mathematics and physics.

Cofler Florica, licentiate in pharmacy, taught drawing and calligraphy.

Stein Richard, high school graduate, taught music.

Brand Sidonia, high school graduate, taught sports.

Schechter David, high school graduate in Hebrew studies, taught Hebrew language.

Reznic Meer, M.D. taught hygiene.

[Page 85]

Administrative and auxiliary staff:

Secretary: Ghertner Avram, licentiate in law.
Deputy Secretary: Horovitz Nadia, high school graduate.
Education Supervisor: Krakauer Charlotte, high school graduate.
Master of crafts: Vigder I. Vigder.
Beniş Carol, member of the law and philosophy teaching staff, was deported to Transnistria, before the school begun.

Kindergarten:

Mrs. Marcus Rivensohn, director.

Miss Rotenberg, assistant.

Miss Tony Avram, assistant.

There was an elementary school in Tg. Dămieneşti, mentioned in 1937.

[Page 86]

C. Charity and Mutual Aid Associations. Additional societies established by Jews

a. Masonic Lodges

The following Masonic lodges have operated in Roman: "Concordia"– Roman, "Lucia"– Bozieni, "Steaua Moldovei" (The Star of Moldova) established in 1882, and "Progresul"– Roman, established and consisted exclusively or mainly of Christians.[1]

In 1873, A.D. Stern mentions the lodge "Fraternitatea" (brotherhood) in the town without any further details.[2] The lodge "Progresul" of the Bnei–Brith order in Roman started operating at the beginning of the 20th century. In 1903, the lodge appealed to the Jewish community in order to collect money, and with the help of a loan from "I.C.A" to start building a school. In 1934, the lodge organized a Jewish celebration in the city. At that time, it had the following officers: M. Forșt, W.L. Schwartz, Noel Bring, A. Laver, Carol Rohrlich, and was presided by H. Haimovici.[3]

In 1886, the charity society "Zion" is mentioned having a ball, whose profits were divided among poor Christians, poor Jews, and the Jewish hospital. The board of the society, (that possibly was a branch of the "Zion" lodge) was composed of Cofman Carol, Luis Șvarț, Carol Rohrlich, Abr. Braunstein, Adolf Axelrad, Isac Abram, Iancu Avram, and M. Berman. The same society held a ball in the next year, with the participation of both Jews and Romanians, and members of the political and administrative leadership of the county. Among the notable Jews who participated, we shall mention I. Moscovici – banker, Max Schiffer – important merchant, Sache Alterescu Buzoianu – attorney and Sigmund Hershcovici. The ball was organized by Saul Dulbergher – the president of the Society, and the members Adolf Axelrad and Marcus A. Iurist. The benefis were given to the poor. The society appointed a committee which, together with the Rabbi of the town would create the means necessary to help the needy, in particular to procure Matzot for Passover.[4]

[Page 87]

b. Mutual Aid Societies

In the "Illustrated Israelite Almanac" of 1903–1904, the following societies in the city, occupied with this topic were mentioned:

"Ahavas Ahim"

"Keisis Israel"

"Reim Akiwes"

"Societatea Damelor pentru ajutorarea femeilor lehuze" (Ladies society for the help of women after birth)

The economic societies "Speranța" (The hope) and "Viitorul" (The future) and the Zionist societies "Cremieux" and "Ahavas Zion." In 1901, the society "Ajutorul Damelor Israelite" (Aid of the Jewish Ladies) is mentioned as well.[5]

In 1921, the mutual aid societies "Fraterna," "Ahavas Ahim," "Reim Ahim," have merged under the name "Fraternitatea." However in 1927, "Fraterna" resumed its independent activities, the following being elected: W.L. Schwartz, Leopold Haimovici, Michel Simișa, Sigmund Baer, Heinrich Leiwandman, Iulius Iștein, Moise Steiu, Iulius Wigder, A.L. Solomon, Pincu Caufman, Moise Iosepovici, Iosef Pinsler, I.I. Cohn, Z.H. Zisman, and Isac Iancovici. The censors were: Max Haimsohn and Aron Rosenberg.[6]

[Page 88]

The association "Ajutor și îndrumare" (Aid and Guidance), was registered in the register of private juridical persons, near the Court of Roman, in 24 Jun 1935.

Extract from the statute of the association

Sec. 2. Intent – Helping the needy Jewish population of Roman, trying to give the opportunity to those declassed or broken, to become working elements, avoiding the situation that brings them to appeal for public compassion.

Sec. 3. The association gives aid by loan, without taking interest, commission or any other payments.

Sec. 4. The maximal help that a needy is granted is 5000 lei. The members of the association are people of both sexes, at the age of least 21 years old.

Funds and dues

The initial contribution of the founding members

The contribution of a new member joining the society.

[Page 89]

Monthly dues of the founding members and all other members (at least 500 Lei per month)

Contribution and subventions of persons or philanthropic institutions.

The organs of the association are:

General Assembly

The administration committee.

The censors' committee.

The administration committee was composed of: prof. J. Koenig, Avram I. Solomon, Iosef Iancovici, Riven Rosenberg, Iosef Stein, Iancu Marcu, Iancu Strul, and Ghidale Marcovici. Censors: B. Bercoff, Sol. Zingher, and Iulius Margulius.[7]

c. Mutual Aid associations of the craftsmen

The society "Cneses Israel" was a mutual aid society for cases of maladies and decease, recognized as a juridical person in 21 Jul 1924. The society was founded in January 1899. The motto in the prologue of the society's statute cites the Talmudist Hama bar Chanina, who describes in poetic mode the intent, or rather part of the goals of the society: "The belief is that people should follow God's example, like Him dressing people, since he dressed Adam and Eve, so you should dress the naked, as He has visited the sick, so you should visit the sick, since He has visited Abraham, when he was sick, as He caresses the saddened, when He comforted Isac when he mourned his parent, you should also caress them, as He buries the dead, since He buried Moses, so you should bury the dead".

[Page 90]

The founding members of the society were: Sucher Cohn, Herman Stanger, H. Rivenzohn, M. Zucker, Simon Lutz, A.S. Segal, Simon Moscovici, A.M. Biderman, D.L. Bercovici, H. Bercovici, Lupu Grunberg, Marcu Segall, David Herşcu, Leon Aranovici, Iulius Aranovici and Ozias Zager.

The management committee for the year 1915–1916: president – Isidor Schiffer, vice presidents – S. Simşensohn and H. Rivensohn, cashier – Lipa I. Spivac, deputy cashier – Meier Weisman, controllers – David Kupferberg and Meier Zucker, signatory – Simon Moscovici, and secretary – Moritz Solomon.

In 1927, Isidor O. Schiffer and H. Rivensohn still held their positions, Solomon Zingher became vice president, Moritz Solomon cashier, Mendel Barasch – secretary and David Kupferberg and Leon Salovici controllers. The tasks and leading organs remained as before. In 1902 the balance of the society was as following:

Income: (taxes, dues, donations) 2611.40 lei.

Expenses: rent – 132 lei, medicines – 698.40, wages 285.70 lei, weekly subventions 245 lei, other subventions 129 lei, office expenses 93.37 lei, commission on the money collection 93.60, wood expenses 25 lei, furniture – 10 lei, other 10.85 lei, overplus – 1759 lei.[8]

"Ahavas Achim" society, like the "Scheins (or Schewes) Achim" contributed to the "progress of Zionist ideas", the first collaborating with the Zionist section "Ahavas Zion." In 1903 they collected money for the National Fund, on the occasion of the general assembly of the Zionist section.[9]

[Page 91]

The association of the barbers' shop owners and workers was founded in 1937 in the city. The president was Alexandru Bucur, one vice president was Milu Flitman, and out of the five censors, two were Jews. There was also an association of barbers and hairdressers.[10]

d. Ladies Associations and Societies

On 31 Oct 1882 the ladies' society "Concordia" was founded in town. At the beginning it had 700 members and a fund of 700 lei. The committee was composed of Mrs. Dr. Reitman, president, A. Rosenstreich, vice president, Schiffer – cashier, Sandman – secretary. As the honorific president was elected Dr. Iosef Taubes. The goal of the society was social assistance.[11]

Since 1922, the documents show the existence of "Asociaţia Culturală a Femeilor Evree" (Cultural association of the Jewish women" ("A.C.F.E"). Most of the activities were of cultural aspect: celebrations, conferences. In 1930 the president was Charlotte Schiffer and the secretary was Rica Horowitz; the association had 252 members. Under its supervision there was a kindergarten with 40 children, two members daily supervised its activity. The Association deployed a rich cultural activity, it had a library, and it organized literature and scientific conferences. It supported the Hebrew course of C.T.S. (Cercul Tineretului Sionist – Jewish youth circle), it gave aid to the unemployed, and it participated in the actions of "Keren Kayemet Le Israel" and "Keren Hayesod." In 1931, it organized the Hanukah party of the kindergarten.[12]

[Page 92]

e. The "Maccabi" Association

In the town and county of Roman, the "Maccabi" association organized rich sports and cultural activities.

The association was founded in 1921, when the following committee was elected:

Suchard Rivensohn – president, Iohan Zisu Zussman – secretary, Tzudic – cashier, Hausvecht and Hutschneker – members.

In 1927 the committee was composed of Lupu Lazăr, Iancu Davidec, R. Stein, Streisfeld, Levi Velt, Curelaru, Blecher, Karmitz and Jean Bayer. In the same year a cyclist section was founded. In the next year, two cultural meetings were held and the association merged with the "Triumph" club.

In 1933, a sports' club "Maccabi" was established at Băceşti – Roman.[13] On 25 and 26 August 1934, a sports' event was held at Roman, with the participation of various sections of "Maccabi", with more than 500 sportsmen.

The event was sponsored by the city council and the Jewish Community of Roman. The festivities started with a parade of all sections in front of the city hall. Opening the parade was the delegation from "Maccabi" Iaşi. From many windows and balconies flowers were thrown at the participants. At the city stadium various sport activities were held: volleyball, soccer, open exercises, running, jumps, pyramids performed by different sections.

[Page 93]

At night, a big party was held in the city park, where the various sections showed open exercises and exercises with instruments. On Sunday, the activity continued at the stadium with tests at semifinals and finals.[14]

Taking into account the beautiful activity deployed for the training of the Jewish youths, the association "Maccabi" received in 1935 a subvention of 2000 lei from the Jewish community (president Att. Cramer and secretary M. Rintzler).[15]

f. The Jewish students association in Roman

In 1927, the committee of the Jewish students was elected: Lupu Leopold – president, members – Leizer Bercu and Katz Lupu.[16]

g. The local sections of the U.E.P. ("Uniunea Evreilor Pământeni" – Native Jews Union) and U.E.R. ("Uniunea Evreilor Români") – Romanian Jews Union

A section of the General association of the Native Jews was founded in Roman in 1891, led by I. Simşen.[17] At the initiative of Iosif Weiss, at the end of December 1903, the section "Deşteptarea" (Awakening) of the "Uniunea Evreilor Pământeni" was re–founded in the city. I. Weiss was elected as the president of the section U.E.P.; He led a fight for the granting of civil rights to the Jews. In 1913, after the start of the Balkan wars, with the participation of Jews in the Romanian army, the fight for granting civil rights started again.

[Page 94]

In February 1913 a general assembly of the U.E.P. local section was held, and a new committee was elected, with Iancu Avram as president, Aron Rosenberg – cashier, Dr. Helfant and Isidor Schiffer vice presidents, and Dr. A. Wexler – controller; secretaries were Suchard Rivenzon and N. Bandel.[18] With the occasion of a conference held under the auspices of U.E.P., several women registered to the section. In 1920, Gabriel Schafer, a student, analyzed critically the political activity of the Jewish population: "In Roman there are two camps, with no understanding among them. One is the U.E.P, under the leadership of Iancu Avram and Isidor Schiffer. The first has worked 30 years for the Jewish well–being, and has given the city a modern school; the second, a man with initiative, watched for the Jewish interests and presided over the distribution of the aid that came through the Joint Distribution committee. Those from the Jewish community, with Laver and Iancu Gross as leaders, were accused of infractions.

As a result, the author of the pamphlet was arrested, being accused of bolshevism, at the suggestion of Iancu Gross. He was released after the intervention of A. Laver, the president of the community.[19]

In 1931 and 1932, discussions of the Jewish Youth, affiliate of the U.E.R, were held in town; at the second one participated the lawyer Iacob Bacalu, the general secretary of the "Tineretului U.E.R" (Youths of U.E.R.) from Bucharest. The topic of the discussions was establishing a local group of the "Tineretului U.E.R"[20]

[Page 95]

D. The Zionist Movement

At the beginning of the 8th decade of the XIXth century, Jews desired to become part of the Romanian society, although there were a series of inconveniences, politico–legal: Art. 7 of the Constitution of 1866, measures against "vagabondism," expulsions, etc., and they still had the benefit of certain economic opportunities, public education, etc.

The 1897 Congress of Basel, where Theodore Herzl envisioned emigration and the founding of a Jewish state in Palestine, then belonging to the Ottoman Empire, was a direct consequence of the anti–Semitic activities in Central and Western Europe, proving thus, that assimilation was not providing a solution.[1]

The first Zionist Society established in the city, called "Chovevei–Zion," in 1893 chose a board composed of: S. Moise Berman – President, Manase Berman and Sam Schlosse – Vice Presidents, Isidor Schiffer – treasurer, Iosef Weiss – Secretary, M.I. Schwartz and Mordhe W. Ruvinsohn – Comptrollers; M. Bring, B. Cofler, Sam Herscovici, Ch. Urband, Meyer Spekter and Manase Segall, members at large. On 21 February, 1899 a meeting of the Society took place in the city, at which its president, Iosef Weise spoke about the scope of Zionism, appealing to the members to subscribe/pledge to the Colonial Bank.

[Page 96]

In two days were pledged over 800 lei.[2]

The society met in April, in the Great Synagogue. Iosef Weiss, M. Braunstein, and I. Goldenthal took the floor. They deliberated on the development of the Zionist movement.[3]

On 18 December, 1899 a Zionist meeting took place, at the same synagogue, speaking was Isac Agent, who lectured on the idea of emigrating to Anatolia.[4] At the 5th World Zionist Congress at Basel, in December 1901, Horia Carp was the delegate on behalf of the Zionists of Roman.[5]

In 1903 a Zionist lecture hall opened in the city, as a result of the efforts of A. Sucher, L. Rapaport, S.S. Cheis (a socialist, probably "Poalei–Zionist") and M. Handman. A. Sucher was elected president of the board. An appeal was launched in view of the increased strength of the Zionist movement.[6] In 1903, Noel Bring was the "Cremieux" and "Ahavas Zion" delegate to the Iaşi conference, and in the same year, Max Nordau represented the Roman

Zionists at the 6th Zionist Congress in Basel.[7] The first wave of emigration from Roman is noted in 1886.[8]

In 1900, emigration continued: 100 Jews departed during the month of May, 50 were determined to travel by foot till Hamburg. The group of pedestrian emigrants arrived to Fălticeni; on 8 June another 64 emigrants departed.[9]

Due to poor crops of that year and the inevitable economic crisis, as a result of which Jews also suffered,

[Page 97]

Th. Herzl wrote to Noel Bring in Vienna: "Intervention is unfortunately impossible. Emigrants must expect the darkest misery in Austria. Please hold them all back. Herzl."[10]

On the 13th of September 1903, a gathering organized by the Zionist sections took place at the Hebrew–Romanian School for Girls in the city. A.S. Rapaport spoke about the decisions of the 6th World Zionist Congress in Basel, in particular about the Jewish colonization of Eastern Africa (Uganda) project. The same issue was touched upon by the city Jewish delegate, Noel Bring.[11]

Regarding emigration we learn the following:

In 1920 an organization for emigration called "Achuza" was founded, in which 35 families registered.[12]

In 1940, the training sites of the local halutzim [pioneers] and of those who came here from other places were:

Work Camp No. 1, Bogdan–Dragoş St. No 123, where they also lived.

Work Camp No. 2, Sucedava St. No 32, where they also lived.

The 52 youths in team no. 1 were 17–20 years of age, from the cities of Moldova, as well as Bucharest and Craiova.[13]

In 1904, at the Hebrew–Romanian School for Girls, the Zionist organizations held a Chanukah celebration. Miss Sophie Davidovici lectured on Zionism and Noel Bring about Theodore Herzl.[14]

[Page 98]

In 1906, the following were elected as delegates from Roman to the "Cultural Conference of Zionists from Piatra Neamţ:" Noel Bring, S.S. Cheiz and A. Sucher ("Egalitatea"/3.II.1906). In 1909, the delegate to the 9th World Zionist Congress was Dr. Helfant, whereas to the Zionist conference of Galaţi,

Noel Bring. Delegates from Roman also participated in the Galaţi Zionist conference on 10 to 11 May, 1915.[15] In 1920, the Zionist organization was lead by Attorney Maximilian Schor.[16]

In 1925, a major Zionist gathering was held at the Great Synagogue in town, which had the objective of expounding on the work of the Zionist Congress of Romania as influenced by "Renaşterea" [Rebirth].[17] In 1929, from the Regional Zionist apparatus for Upper Moldova was selected W.L. Schwartz from Roman.[18]

In 1941, Davidovici Iosif, commercial clerk from Băceşti–Roman, was deported to Tg. Jiu on account of Zionist activities. Nevertheless, in 1942, the Zionist organization requested and obtained renewal of activities, on behalf of Mr. Radu Lecca. Members of the committee were: Mr. M. Reznic – President and Leo Rohrlich, Rabbi Mendel Frenkel, Iosub Leizerovici and Solomon Sabo, members.[19]

Zionist Divisions for Adults

In 1899, in the village of Bara–Roman the Zionist organization "Ohavei Zion," Dr. C. Lippe unit, was founded, with an initial membership of 52.[20] In 1902 the unit "Ahavas Zion" is mentioned, which partially replaced, and completed the policy of the old "Chovevei–Zion" guard by purchasing land, funded by the collection of "shekels" (funds for building up the national homeland). The meeting took place at the site of the local Society "Ahavas Achim". The talk was about "the ninth day of Av and the dispersion of the Jews" and about "the need for Zionism". In December 1902 it celebrated Chanukah at the Jewish School for Boys, together with the unit "Cremieux". They lit candles, they sang and speeches were made by Noel Bring, A.S. Rapaport, Simon S. Cheiz and Moses Handman. A fundraiser was made for J.N.F. (Keren Kayemet LeIsrael).

[Page 99]

In February 1903 a general meeting of the unit was held at the site of the Society "Ahavas Achim". A. Avramovici spoke about "Zionism". The speech was followed by a discussion on cultural activities, in which participated: M. Handman, Noel Bring, A. Avramovici. Funds were raised for the J.N.F. In the same month another meeting was held at the same place. M.M. Krieghel spoke about "ritual killing" and Noel Bring about "Philanthropic Zionism" and "The Zionist philanthropy."

The Zionist units "Ahavas Zion" and "Cremieux" organized a series of activities like fundraising, lottery, to help the poor population. The programs were initiated by Solomon Kofler, the Vice President of the unit, helped by Marie Gropper.

In July 1903, the unit organized a conference, featuring M. Handman, about "The vitality of the Jewish nation," he also spoke in August about "Pericope of the week," The "accusation of ritual killing," "New York and Jerusalem." The first conferences were held at the"Bais Hadaş" synagogue, and the last one at the unit's headquarters. Noel Bring wished him success on behalf of the community, upon his departure to America to pursue rabbinical studies. The "Ahavas Zion" and "Cremieux" units organized a banquet with the occasion of M. Handman's departure.

[Page 100]

On 27 June 1904, the same two units organized a requiem at the "Moşke" Synagogue in memory of Th. Herzl. The following spoke: Sol. Laufer, A.S. Rapaport, S.S. Cheiz, L. Weissbuch, Noel Bring and I. Goldenberg.

The "Cneses Israel" Society mailed a letter of condolences to Vienna.[21]

The "H. Rosenbaum" Zionist unit was founded on 1 May, 1906, with 35 members. Its president, M. Schweitzer and its secretary H. Rosner issued the following communiquÃ©: The committee's meetings are held every Wednesday, regularly; the membership grew by 10 members; on the 2nd of July a requiem was organized in memory of Th. Herzl, a protest rally was held against the Bialystok massacres. The following spoke: L. Honig and Noel Bring; during the month several lectures were given, among them those of professors A. Rapaport and A. Suchar. On the 8th of July, Ire Keiss lectured at the Great Synagogue, of the tailors.

In December 1906 the united sections of "Cremieux" and "H. Rosenbaum" organized festivities of Chanukah at the Hebrew School for Boys, Noel Bring and Dr. Henic showed the significance of the holiday, comparing the Zionists with the Maccabean from the time of the Hasmoneans, demonstrating that the Zionist movement was the only capable of resolving the Jewish problem.

[Page 101]

On the 6th of January, 1908 the Zionist unit "H. Rosenbaum" was re-established. The newly voted committee was composed of: S. Solomon – President, and I. Weisselberg, Isac Iancovici, Benglas Zwicker and M. Grunberg.

The following year it also organized a Chanukah celebration, the following spoke: S. Solomon, A. Sucher, Dr. Helfant and Noel Bring.[22]

In 1921 the Zionist group "Th. Herzl" was mentioned, including about 300 older members, with activities limited to fund raising.[23]

Youth Zionist Organizations

On 11 April, 1899 a gathering of Jewish youth was held at the home of A. Liberman. On this occasion, a new unit of "B'nei Zion" was founded; its committee was composed of: Noel Bring – President, A. Liberman – Vice President, Isac Stein – comptroller and I. Keiss – Secretary.

In April the unit adopted the name "Cremieux", in honor of the Jewish French leader Isac Adolphe Cremieux, holding on the 24th day of April a general meeting where S.S. Keiz, the secretary of the society spoke about "The rescue of the Jewish people through Zionism"; C. Goldenthal deliberated on the topic "The evolution of modern Zionism from 1894 to the second Congress of Basel"; A. Segall spoke about the "importance of Jewish resettlement of Eretz Israel". The gathering was concluded by the president of the unit N. Bring.

[Page 102]

On the 3rd of May the final committee of the "Cremieux" unit was elected. It was composed of Noel Bring – President, A. Segall and A.I. Lieberman – Vice Presidents, Zigmund I. Goldstein – treasurer, S.S. Cheiz – First Secretary, H. Leport – Second Secretary, H.I. Bercovici and Jacques Zinger – advisory members.

At the general meeting of the 5th of May the following spoke: Noel Bring discussed the necessity of the Zionist struggle and the nurture of national history and language as the means of awakening national sentiment, Stein spoke about the lore/legends of the Jewish people; Leport about the current state of the Jews. On the 15th day of May the following lectured: I. Goldenthal – the principal of the Jewish school, about the Jewish character, and S.S. Cheiz.

In June, the activity of the unit was maintained through regular meetings on Saturdays, Zionist lectures, and the course of Jewish history given by Professor I. Goldenthal. The first collection of 35 "shekels" was initiated at the center. Th. Herzl congratulated the new committee for its activities and accepted the honorary presidency of the unit.

In September, at the Great Synagogue a Zionist gathering took place, at which the following spoke: Noel Bring, A. Segall and Sigmund Goldstein. They debated problems connected to the development of the Zionist movement in the city.

In November at the same location, another gathering was held. Dr. Henic spoke about the significance of the study of Jewish history and the Hebrew language. Noel Bring, the President spoke about the Zionist movement and the significance of the Colonial Bank, the students A. Segall and Sigmund Goldstein spoke as well.

[Page 103]

A new committee was elected: Noel Bring – President, Simon S. Cheiz and Sigmund Baer – Vice Presidents, Sigmund I. Goldenberg – Treasurer, Nathan Zalman – Comptroller, Osias M. Zagar – Secretary, Moritz Bercovici and Solomon Prialnic (Priacnic?) – Advisory Members.

On 14 December, 1902, the unit organized a Chanukah celebration. On 20 July, 1903 a gathering was held at the Great Synagogue, by the "Cremieux" and "Ahavas Zion" units. Noel Bring, committee member of the Zionist Federation, opened the meeting. Dr. Leon Ghelber (Vienna) spoke about a modern 9th of Av, relative to the events in Chişinău, underlining that the rescue of the Jewish population can happen only in Zion. Moses Handman spoke about the 9th of Av, from a historic point of view. A fundraiser was held for the JNF.

Noel Bring, born in 1874 in Roman, was a personality of the Jewish world, thanks to his efforts in the philanthropic arena and Zionist propaganda. He founded the "Cremieux" Zionist Society, whose president he was. He was at the helm of the local community and Vice President of the Society "Cneses Israel." He was a supporter of Jewish emigration.[24]

On the 28th of September 1899, a Zionist association of young Jewish women, called "B'noth Sion" was founded, with the support of the "Cremieux" group. The founding meeting was presided by the local Zionist leader, Noel Bring. On the 3rd of October a committee was elected: Fanny Leibovici – President, Bella Hausknecht and Marie Honigsberg – Vice Presidents, Etty Avramovici – Treasurer, Marie Rosenberg – Comptroller, Clementine Honigsberg – Secretary, Mathilde Tzimand – Assistant, Debora Fillerman (Filderman?) and Clara Prinacnic – Counselors. At Noel Bring's proposal, it was decided that the group should be named after the Zionist fighter from New

York – Professor Emma Gotheil. On the 10th of October 1899, the gathering of the feminine Society "Gotheil" took place at the local Jewish school. The following spoke: Miss Hausknecht about "The role of women in different times and their Zionist duty" and Noel Bring, about "The contemporary status of women."

[Page 104]

In February 1904, a series of lectures by Eremia Grunstein, speaker of the Zionist Federation Committee of Galaţi, was held. In Roman there were three lectures: two at the "Bait Chodoş" (Moşke) Synagogue and one at the Great Synagogue (on the days of 7th and 8th of February).

On this occasion, the foundations were set for a Zionist association of women and girls. "Shekels" were sold and funds were raised for the JNF.

In March of 1904 the committee of the Zionist unit, "B'nos Zion Emma Gotheil" was elected:

Marie Scharaga – President, Frida Akerman – Vice–President, Clara Schwartz – Treasurer, Eva Rapaport – Secretary, Renee Zisman – Comptroller, Mina Margulis and Rebecca Mayr – Advisors.[25]

Under the influence of certain young Zionists a lectures club was founded.[26]

In 1915, thanks to the initiative of several young people and following discussions held by Ira Keiss, the Zionist unit "Or Zion" was established, with a Borochov orientation. The youths were especially active in physical/athletic education.

[Page 105]

Funds were raised for the purchase of gymnastic equipment. Neither the political nor the cultural aspects were neglected. Funds were raised for the JNF. The unit had a library of Judaic literature.[27]

In 1927, a young Zionist circle was founded, called "Avodah," led by Schiffer. In February of the following year, at the "Avodah" circle A. Mibashan lectured on the "Origins of the Jewish People". Iulius Schaffer, President of the Zionist organization in the city, P. Weifel and B. Karpin spoke as well.[28]

In January 1928, the organization "Haşomer Haţair" of Roman organized at Dămieneşti, a Chanukah festival. In March 1928, a memorial was held for the Jewish fighter Yosef Trumpeldor. I. Rosenfeld spoke about his life and fight.

Part of this organization was also the well–known physician Joseph Fux, the author of "Surgery of the Pancreas", published in Editura Medicală, Bucharest, 1957.

Joseph Fux was born in a modest home on 15th March, 1913, son of Moişe Fux, he was named Iosef (Joseph ben Moşe Hacohen).

During the third year of high school he joined the Zionist movement as a member of the "Haşomer Haţair" organization where he polished his knowledge of Hebrew and led a very active life which brought him to positions of leadership of the organization, along with his colleagues, Marcu Grunberg and Mayer Iosupovici.[29]

About the "Circle of the Zionist Youth" (C.T.S.) of Roman we learn from the 1928 writings of the student Sami Wecsler. After that, C.T.S. had the role of revitalizing, within limits, the local Jewish cultural life.

[Page 106]

The author wished that the second brochure published that year should be the beginning of the activity of those capable to educate Jewish masses, by starting a monograph of the community.

In 1940, Iancuşor Schwartz passed away; he was member of the "Hasmoneea" Committee from 1929 to 1930 and vice president between 1930 and 1931. Born into a Zionist family in Roman, he belonged to the Zionist wing of A.G.S.E. (Asociaţia Generală a Studenţilor Evrei = General Association of the Jewish Students) and the "Hasmoneea" Society.[30]

In 1921, Jewish pupils' Zionist organization "Agaezul Macabeii" is mentioned.[31]

All Zionist and Jewish organizations and associations contributed to the JNF (Jewish National Fund) and "Keren Hayesod."

In this regard we shall mention some of these contributions. In 1903, M. Froimovici raised funds for JNF, in 1908, the "H. Rosenbaum" unit raised money for both funds. In 1921, "Comisariatul Fondului Naţional" [the Committee of the National Fund] was active in Roman under the leadership of Leopold Haimovici and Alfred Herscovici.

In 1922, fund raising activities for the benefit of these organizations were intensified. In 1925, in only two days they raised in the city 400,000 lei.

In 1928, in Dănieneşti, they organized "Comisariatul N.F.E." [JNF Committee] headed by Solomon Rosenfeld.

To promote these activities, the following participated: B. Karpin (Berlin), M. Segal (Chişinău), I. Smoira (Tel Aviv) and Dr. D. Wilenski.

[Page 107]

In May 1940, "Hagalil" and "Keren Kayemet" actions were initiated with the participation of a special delegate from Jerusalem headquarters, Rabbi Roth. Also active were Attorney B. Caushanski from Iaşi, Mina Haimovici and I. Leizerovici, the director of JNF of Roman.

In 1942, even though the Zionist Organization was reactivated, it was forbidden to raise money for these funds. (see also "Neamul evreiesc" [Jewish Nation], year XIV no. 23–24/ 16.X. 1921, "Mântuirea" [Redemption] year III/no. 944/26.II.1922, "Renaşterea" [Rebirth], year I no. 28/29.III.,1925, "Ştiri din viaţa evreiască" [News from the Jewish Life] 27.III.1926, "Egalitatea" [Equality] 9.III.1928, "Ştiri din lumea evreiască" [News from Jewish World] 15.I.1928).

[Page 108]

E. Aspects of the Spiritual Life of the Jews in Roman and Surroundings

The spoken language of the Roman Jews was Yiddish, yet they also spoke the Romanian language, some – the Russian and German languages, all a function of the country from which they have emigrated and came to Moldova, and particularly, to the old county of Roman.

In various documents, they carry Romanian names or names adapted from Yiddish in the Romanian language from early on. Thus, we encounter names such as: Cercu [circle], Lupu [wolf], Ariton, but in the documents they nevertheless signed with the Hebrew name.

Certain names derive, as I've already shown, from the occupations of their predecessors: Stoleru [carpenter], Sticlaru [glazier], Tejetaru. We encounter many names, Hebrew or Yiddish in origin, which have been "Romanianized" through the addition of suffixes used in Romanian.

Aron, Aroneanu, Aronovici or Aronescu. Abram, Abramovici, Avramescu. In fact, a name like Aroneanu or Aronovici is actually Ben Aharon [son of Aharon], the same in many other cases. Some names are encountered in various forms, sometimes difficult to identify. Baruch is also called Burăh, Baroh or Benedict. Certain Germanic names are similarly used in numerous forms: Schwartz can also be Şvart. Edelstein can be also called: Adelstain. The same name can be written in different forms or spellings, preserving either the German form: 'Sch' or transforming it into (the Romanian) 'Ş'; names with (the German) 'W' are often used with 'V'; instead of 'K', 'C' has taken over. Maier can become: Mayr, Meir, Meer or Mayer, etc.

[Page 109]

The German 'ei' diphthong becomes 'ai' (Beinglas becomes Bainglas). Names, such as: Cofler become Coflea and GrÃ¼nberg transforms into Grinberg or Grimberg. A certain document mentions a Jewish soldier fallen in WWI, whose name was Ţifui – a specifically Romanian name. It is possible that this soldier's predecessors were called Ţvi.

In documents, a curious–enough compound of Hebrew and Romanian is used at the end of the 19th century (see the notations in the Roman Pinkas [register] from that period).

But the Hebrew language was used not only by the Rabbis in the synagogue. In the *Heider* and *Talmud–Tora* and later, in the Hebrew–Romanian schools, which have appeared particularly after the restrictive law of 1897, the Hebrew language has occupied a frontal place; remarkable "Hebraists," such as: Zalman Schachter, Berl Brucar or Ghidale Marcovici have come out of Roman's Jewish/Hebrew schools.[1]

There existed also journalists and writers who expressed themselves perfectly in the Romanian language; Jews have always considered speaking the language of one's native or adoptive country a necessity.

The conduct of the Moldovan (Moldavian) Jews was, according to Kaufman, the Romanian–Oriental conduct at the beginning of the 19th century. Girls used to wear their hair plaited and were letting it hang over their heads, like the Moldavian girls. The women used to cut their hair and tie their heads, the old women used to wear a doublet with silver threads on their chest. A document from the end of the 18th century, mentions ornamental objects: "a Jew of Roman pawned pearls and ornaments that the Jewesses put on their heads". The dressing style used by Jews was according to their country of origin: "the Galician" style, or the "Iashian" (from the city of Iaşi) style, which was worn particularly by Hassidim. At the beginning of the 19th century, the "German" dressing style was characteristic of those who had come from Western or Central Europe and which, toward the end of that century, became general. A specifically Jewish habit was wearing hats and, in general, covering the head in any environment, particularly in the synagogue.[2]

[Page 110]

A great deal can be said about the rules in the area of food matters. We shall only mention some of the specific dishes: *humentaş* (Purim cake), *ghefilte fiş* (stuffed fish), *kugel* etc.

Something about the Jewish folklore: for Purim, children used to sing and dance the *"Purimşpil"* [Purim Play], using a rattler. Here is an excerpt from such a play, selected by Yulian Shvarts:

> *"A good Purim, a good Purim, my dear*
> *You don't know what Purim means?*
> *Purim means giving money to the poor*
> *I come in hopping with my little bare feet*
> *I'd begin singing to you but my need is too great*
> *Let my soul be blessed, pay me my dues*

Do not let me stay here. I'm going, falling
My beard is big, my wife is sick..."

[Page 111]

Text: [Romanian translation of the above] – collected in Roman.[3]

Haralamb Zincă remembers the beautiful Jewish legends told by the talented professor Iosif Feldstein.[4]

Interesting is also the way the Jew was regarded in the local Romanian folklore. At the beginning of the 20th century, the play: "Gypsy Wedding" was running in Roman; the play was grotesque at times, sometimes too folkloristic in its language. The dressing was ordinary, but sometimes grotesque, even vulgar... Using this play as a model, the play: "Jewish Wedding", was composed in the twenties in Roman. It was the same in style, language and spirit as its predecessor.[5]

Recently, Andrei Oisteanu reminded us of Lazăr Şaineanu's opinion, but especially that of Moses Schwartzfeld's, with regard to this problem: "It (the study) brings out the Jew with the qualities and flaws that the Romanian sees in him, but at the same time he will unveil, at least in part, the power of observation, the prejudices and the weaknesses of the Romanian people (...); the Romanian will depict the Jew as he sees, believes and understands him, but not as he was or is in reality". Much sharper, regarding this problem, are certain scholars who have psychoanalyzed the collective unconscious of the Christians: "The characteristics attributed to the Jew in the anti–Semitic folklore have nothing to do with the real Jew but with the Christians who have initiated those attributes. If the folklore is an autobiographic ethnography then, the anti–Semitic folklore says a great deal about Christians and hardly anything about Jews".[6]

[Page 112]

Writing about popular Jewish art, Iţic Kara mentions the ornaments of the Aron Kodeş [Holy Ark] in the Central Synagogue in Roman, as well as the Pinkasim [Registers]. Unfortunately, with the old cemetery destroyed in 1872, it is impossible anymore to admire the art of the Jewish stone carvers.[7]

Moise Lax mentions the visit of Velvl Zbarjer, the miraculous troubadour of those times (the beginning of the 20th century), in Roman. In the city, Iacob Psantir had nephews who were musicians. The figures of Ignatz Polypody, who had come from Kiev, and the cantor M. Kivilevici, who lived a certain period of time here, are also worth mentioning. In the first decade of the 20th century, the great Yiddish–language writer Șalom Aleichem visited the city.[8]

Books, magazines, newspapers and other official Jewish publications of Roman authors published in Roman

A.V. Nerson – *Romanian Jews in the 20th century – Reflections over the matter of Jews in Romania*, Roman 1910

[Page 113]

Suchard Rivenson – *The Jewish school in Roman*, printed at Beram Sr. (the father) Press, 1933

Rabbi Isaia, Avraham Ben–Israel – *Chehilas Israel* [Jewish community], Hebrew

Hatope, Roman 1980 Hebrew

Hai Israel [The Jewish people is alive], Roman, 1904 Hebrew

Haor [The light], Roman 1904

A.S. Rapaport, *Soșan Iacov* Hebrew

A.S. Rapaport *Ester Hamalca* [Queen Esther] Hebrew

"Der folks Dolmetscher" [The folk translator, interpreter], Roman 1891, Yiddish

Humăntaș [Purim cake], Roman 1900 Yiddish

Der Griner Culsman Yiddish

Der Gragăr [the Purim rattle] Yiddish

Der Parăh [nasty, offensive, fellow] Yiddish

"Școala nouă" [The new school], Roman, 1900 Yiddish

"Gazeta Balului" [newspaper of the ball], 1933

"Emigranții Romanului" [the emigrants in Roman], 1900

Strigăt de disperare [a cry of despair], Roman 1900

"Apelui femeilor evreice din Roman" [appeal of the Jewish women in Roman], Roman, 1900

Statutele Comunității Israelite din Roman [Statutes of the Jewish community], Roman 1905

Idem, Roman, 1926, Beram Sr. (the father) Press

Idem, Roman, 1936

"Statutele Societăţii meseriaşilor" [Statutes of the Craftsmen's Society], "Cneses Israel [Jewish Community]" Roman, "Viitorul" Press – Leon Grunberg, 1927

Statutul sinagogii "Bais Iancov" (the shoe makers synagogue)

Macabi", Roman, 1938

[Page 114]

"Buletinul comisiei centrale sioniste din Roman", Roman, 1920 weekly, 2 pages

"Ierusalim" – Buletinul comisiei centrale sioniste din Roman [Jerusalem – The Bulletin of the Central Zionist Committee of Roman]

The publications appearing in 1900 were intended as assistance for immigrants. They have appeared in a single copy. "Der folks Dolmetscher" has been subtitled: a publication for families, commerce and all the Jewish problems.

In his micro–monograph, Sami Wecsler asserts that he has published two brochures with respect to the history of the Jews.

At the end of the 19th century, Iancu Gross of Roman is collaborating, with articles and correspondence, in "Egalitatea"; in the local newspaper "Romanu", some of his translations from the German language appear: "*Ioan Halgado si moartea*" [Ioan Halgado and Death], "*Oarba si fiica eĩ*" [The blind woman and her daughter] etc. Professor Suchard Rivenzon collaborates in the "Curierul Israelit. "The publicist H. St. Streitman collaborates in the magazine "Şcoala nouă" appearing in Roman.

The love of books of the Roman Jews is emphasized, as well as the "prenumerants," who support the appearance of certain works, as *Divrei haiamim learţot derumenie* [History of Romania] by I. Psantir (from Demieneşti, Alter Mendelsohn from Roman, Nisen Schwartz, Bernat Schwartz and David Gross) or the *Noua carte a predicilor* [The new book of the preachers] appearing in 1937 in Iaşi by Rabbi Sam Şvemer (with the contribution of Iehuda Leib ben Iţhok Grinberg – the president of the community, his brother Abraham ben Iţhok Grinberg, B. Brucăr, Iosef Neuman and Şlomo Beriş).

[Page 115]

Iacob Iosif Romaner, originating, as its name suggests, from the city, published in Ploieşti the play: *Estera or the assimilated and Zionists.*[9]

"Illustrated post cards" publishing houses were known in the city: the publishing and printing shop "Viitorul", Leon Grunberg, 1909–1916; "Cooperative bookshop", Rotenberg, 1904; the publishing house "The Schools' Bookshop", I. Beram; "The Publishing house, bookshop and stationery", Roman, Michel Schimsensohn, 1929–1941; the publishing house "Cooperative Bookshop", brothers Rottenberg, 1899–1914.[10]

Iţik Kara mentions that Jewish print shops existed in the city in the 19th century. In the next century, besides the above–mentioned printers, there were those who belonged to Leon Friedman, Isidor Grunberg, Herş M. Abramovici and Rivensohn Calman.

The following owned bookshops: Ozias Beram, Brizel Solomon in Roman and Weisman Abel in Băceşti. The following journalists lived and published in the city: Moscovici Bercu and Somer Nathan, A.V. Nerson and others.

The writer Max Belcher, who died in 1938, lived in Roman for a while. Also connected to the town are the names of Aharon Blumenfeld (Ronetti–Roman), Haralamb Zinca (Hary–Zilberman) of "The King of reporting", Filip Brunea–Fox, the writer Solo Har–Herescu, etc.

In the years 1918–1922, the following libraries operated in town: "Ronetti–Roman" and "Or Zion". The library of the "Maccabi" Society functioned between 1920 and 1935, while the A.C.F.E. library started operating in 1925, and was later transformed into the community library. The Rozenberg library, which carried Jewish and didactic books, was founded in 1920. The following synagogues also contained Jewish libraries: "Rabi Leivi" (300 volumes), "The Central Synagogue", "Zalmino", "The Leipzigher synagogue", etc. The library "Iosif Neulicht" was opened in 1937 at the Hebrew School, in memory of the former school principal.

[Page 116]

Libraries were owned also by the cultural societies "Ierusalim", "Amiciţia" and "Steuerman–Rodion." In 1926, the Jewish youth from the Băceşti community founded a cultural circle and a library. The cultural circle was led by the young women Simon, Benes, Abramovici and Almer and the young men Weserman, Smertzler, Rabinovici and Istric.[11]The library of the Hebrew School (Iosif Neulicht) contained 1288 volumes. In 1940, the foundation of the Jewish High School library in the city started from the donations: Rosenberg (51 Hebrew books and 2 in Yiddish), I. Neulicht (elementary school), Iosef Stein (150 volumes, literature books), Iancu Ghelberg (200 volumes of didactic and scientific literature). In 1942, the library consisted of 688 volumes: 561 in Romanian, 2 in Yiddish, 61 in Hebrew, 118 in German, 26 in French, 8 in Latin and 6 in Greek. One book had the autograph of Max Blecher. Of the rare books, we shall mention: Solomon Gessner – *Der Todt Abels* [Abel's Death], 1795; Albrecht von Geller – *Versuch Schweitzerische gedichte* [Swiss Poems], 1753 and Neuman *Die Ziegel Fabrikation* [the brick production, 1874.[12]

There was always a particular preoccupation with the study of the Hebrew and Yiddish languages, as well as the history of the Jews. In 1903, a circle of Hebrew language and literature study was established. Among the circle members were: A. Sucher, M. Handman, A. S. Rapaport, S. Ghelber and others. In June 1922, the Yiddish celebration of Hebrew poetry took place, with the participation of the following people of letters: Gala Galaction, Eliezer Steinberg and Iacob Botoshanski. In 1926, an evening course of religion, Jewish history and Hebrew language was started for students of state–schools.[13]

[Page 117]

In 1943, there had been a demand for the creation of a seminary course of Judaism, following which, students between the ages of 12 and17, graduated of a few secondary classes, were recruited; both the language and history of the Romanians was taught.

In the Jewish disciplines, the following have been invited to teach: Rabbi Mendel Frenkel, I. Neuman, S. Dimant, H. Leivandman and Zalman Schachter. The curriculum was the following: Hebrew language and literature; The *Bible and Talmud*, with commentaries; ancient and modern history of the Jews; Introduction to the *Talmud* through the *Mishna*; Synagogue music; Our legislation; Religious ethics and morals.[14]

The preoccuuage with the Hebrew language was still pointed out in 1948, when the Roman professors Isacsohn Debora and Iţic participated in the professors' course on Judaic studies, being held in Piatra Neamţ.[15]

Various Jewish associations, clubs and societies have also had cultural programs, organizing celebrations, social events and conferences.

Thus, in 1903, L. Weisbuch held a conference on a Biblical subject, dwelling on the role that culture and solidarity must play among Jews.[16]

[Page 118]

Here are a few of the conferences of cultural character:

A. Sucher – "The Lamentations of Jeremiah" (1903)

Dr. Leon Henic – "About the Vitality of the Jewish People"

A. Sucher – "The Ancient and Modern Maccabees

S.S Cheiz – "The Importance of the Holiday and Celebration of Hanukah

A.S. Rapaport – "National Movements, Ancient and Modern"

Gottfried Margulies – "The French Revolution"

Dr. L. Henic – "The Blood Circulation"

Charlotte Is. Schiffer – "The Role of the Jewish Women in the Movement of the native Jews" (1913 – *U.E.P.*)

D. Hershcovici (Iaşi) – "Yehudah Ha'Levi"

Bercu Iosif – Der Declamator (The Reciter)

Dr. M. Singer – "The Jews in the Works of Anatole France"

Att. Arn. Cramer – "The Jewish Genius in Religion and Philosophy" (1925)

Barbu Lazareanu – "From the Series of Barbu Lazareanu" (1926)

Richard Stein – "Jewish Music"

Suchard Rivenzon – "The Jews in the French Literature" (Edmond Fleg) 1928

Att. S. Marcovici – "The Legislation of the Jews"

Prof. Weisberg – "Heroism of the Jews" (1928)

Prof. I. Konig – "Nathan the Wise"

Prof, Abr. Hollinger – "Baruch Spinoza"[18]

[Page 119]

The most appreciated cultural events were the theatrical performances. In 1888, a group of youths have performed the play *Corban Bairam* (The Bairam) by Moshe Horowitz. In the same year, there have been more theater shows such as: "Marfăgiu [merchant] or the Emigration of Jews to America" (adapted from "The Emigrants" by Şaikevici–Sumer, "The Charmer" [The Sorceress] by Avram Goldfaden.[19]

In 1903, the "Leiblich" drama group performed the play "Hadassa" by Moşe Horowitz, and in the following year, the Jigniţa Theater operetta troupe performed the operettas: "Blimale" or "Pearl of Warsaw" by Iosif Lateiner and "*Ecoul Armatei*" [Echo of the Army] by Zigmund Feinmann.[20]

Because of the lack of theater halls, Roman was very rarely visited by the troupes on tour. In the summer of 1922, the "Schwartz" Garden, renovated by the new entrepreneur, Isac Herşcovici, re–opened. Led by the actor Nottara, the Bucharest National Theater group of artists performed a show.[21]

In 1928, a group of young people performed "Oilom Hatoi" and the Haşomer Haţair presented a program with a few plays directed by Ghedale Marcu.[22]

In the 30s of the 20th century, the Herman Yablokoff American troupe visited the city and a group of amateurs performed the play: "Orfelina". In 1933, the "Gan" children preformed at the Modern Theater the plays: "*Shilgiyah*" [Snow–White] and "The Flower Hora".[23]

[Page 120]

Roman's Jews have given birth to some remarkable musical personalities: here were born Gina Şaraga Solomon and Richard Stein (born in 1909).

Richard Stein first taught music at the Israelite–Romanian school, and from 1940, at the local Jewish high–school.

In 1942, the artist organized and conducted a concert of Jewish music. The following year his father died, and he and his sister Rita addressed the Governor the following request:

"Our Father died in Bârlad and we are called telegraphically to assist with the burial and with the ritual procedures. We are the only children of the deceased. We're asking you to approve."

The author of the hit "Sanie cu Zurgălăi" [A Sleigh with Horses] died in 1992.[24]

Plastic arts were represented by the artist A. Gropeanu and the architect Marcel Locar.

[Page 121]

F. The Jews of Roman and the Jewish Problem
in the Local and National Press

Public Thanks

("Romanu", Roman 9 May 1885)

"On the 5th of the current month, while I was passing over the Moldova Bridge, Mr. Herşcu Calman, the bridge's warden changed for me a bill of 100 lei. Being in a hurry, I forgot on his table my purse containing another 100 lei and various valuable papers. It didn't take long after I arrived to my house, and Mr. Calman, following me with his carriage, found me and returned me my purse. For this laudable deed, I feel that I need to thank and honor publicly Mr. Calman, and be forever grateful.

Peter G. Misir."

From: *The Jewish problem* in A.V. Nerson – *Romanian Jews in the 20th century – Reflections on the Jewish Issue in Romania*, Roman 1910. Printing House Leon Friedman.

Extracts:

"The idea that Jews are rich is wrong, a prejudice. In many of the towns of Moldova, Buhuşi, Neamţ, Focşani, you will find, in a population of 34,000 Jews, 2 – 3 rich people, 1,300 small merchants, the rest being poor laborers. The 200–300 merchants that own a shop look rich; however, in reality they live from today to tomorrow, have to pay rent, a policy etc., but in order to keep their credit in order, they do everything they can just to preserve the appearance of wealthy merchants. The majority of the Jews are small manufacturers or craftsmen: shoemakers, tailors, tinsmiths. Jews are involved not just in commerce.

[Page 122]

Many of the Jews are craftsmen. Until 15–20 years ago, most of the tailors and shoemakers were Jews, and if so many of them became merchants, it was not their fault. Since the old days, commerce was the only way of living they were allowed to practice freely, and it is clear that practicing it for centuries, they improved and became good and able merchants. They could have been good farmers, good engineers and lawyers, if only they were allowed to be...

The law has expelled them from the rural communities, motivated by the fact the *Jidan* (pejorative word for Jew) exploits the peasant, tempts him into drinking and cheats him in measures. An inexperienced person may have thought that as soon as the Jews were expelled from the villages, happiness will prevail in the rural communities. However, the experience proved this assertion to be false. Since 20 years ago, as the Jews left the villages and the pubs were transferred into Christian hands, the misery remained the same as in the past, the alcoholism has not disappeared and the poor peasants had the only consolation of being exploited not by a Jew but by a Romanian brother, if it wasn't an Armenian or a Greek...

The fact is that the Jew, possessing good qualities, can easily adapt to new fields of activities: The Romanian families and the Romanian aristocracy are hiring Jews for managing their estates and factories, as well as doing their book keeping, and although they would like to hire a Romanian worker, their particular interest drives them, sometimes with regret, to hire a Jew as the head of their establishment. We all know the Romanian families that are involved in intensive agriculture, in manufacturing conserves, exploiting forests, in the timber business, or that they have oil wells, and it is a fact that Jews are placed at the head of those modern establishments. Nevertheless, every year during Easter, the Christians exploit the hate against the "Jidans," because the traitor Judah Iscariot was one of them.

[Page 123]

Neither the Spanish Inquisition and the massacres against Jews of ages ago, nor the more sophisticated persecutions, but of the same cruelty level, of the present days were enough to expiate the ancient sin in the eyes of the Christians, thus even nowadays we suffer, for the 300 – 400th generation, the consequences of an ignoble but individual act, done by one of our own... Christ was a Jew, who commanded nothing but to love your fellow man as you love yourself. How can your conscience cope with the inhuman measures you are taking against those of your own God's nation? How can you conciliate your deeds with His sublime morals?

The French journalist Hardouin has affirmed: "Nothing can be done without God's will. It was the Father's will that the Son, Jesus Christ, be betrayed by one of his disciples. None of the apostles hurried to carry God's will and betray. It was Judah who sacrificed himself and decided to be the first martyr of Christianity, and with a bleeding heart he betrayed, and he carried on with his self–sacrifice, until he degraded himself by taking the 30 dinars as payment for the betrayal."

[Page 124]

Anghel Corbeanu – *Max Blecher* ("R.C.M." 1 Jan 1972)

"Born on 8 September 1909 in Botoşani, M. Blecher comes from a middle class Jewish family. His father was a well off merchant who kept a porcelain shop on the main street of Roman, where the products of a small ceramics factory (Lazăr), located at the outskirts of the town, were displayed and sold. He left the city of Botoşani to Roman as a child, studied there in the elementary school and high–school, growing up in the atmosphere of a provincial town, which generated the poetry of obsession of Bacovia (...)

From 1928, at the age of 19, M. Blecher's tragedy began – a life as an infirm, living the rest of his life on his back, immobilized. However, the terminally ill youngster was a lively intellectual, interested in literature, philosophy and painting.

On wheeled tables placed at the left and the right of his bed, where his ivory hands could reach – notes his friend Saşa Pană, who visited him many times – were placed the current books and journals, sent from abroad (...). After wandering in various sanatoriums for bones tuberculosis, in the spring of 1935, M. Blecher's parents rented for their son a quiet house at the outskirts of Roman.

[Page 125]

Here he wrote at all times, carrying out his vocation until his last moment. This was the way Saşa Pană surprised him, writing in the same position he ate and slept, with the notebook placed on a plank, fit on his knees, bent by ankylosis. This was the way Mihail Sebastian found him, and will never forget the big eyes, a little glassy, dilated by the long insomnia, the quiet voice, sometimes sticky from unshed tears..."

Engineer Ion Uscatu – "Remembrance – *Righteous among people – A name for eternity – Viorica Agarici*"

"3 July 1941 – A freight train arrives to the station, with the cars locked and guarded by soldiers. Viorica Agarici was already accustomed to such trains, from which prolonged moans were heard. But she is stopped by soldiers, carrying rifles with bayonets on top. Little did she know that this train was one of the two "death trains", departed from Iaşi three days ago with the destination Călărași. But Viorica was not a person to be frightened, not even by bayonets. She stopped in front of the train, and warned the soldiers that she will break the doors open, to see what is happening inside, and what is the reason for the moans and screams.

The guards, Romanians or Moldovans, became frightened by such daring, and although they were afraid of punishment, they let her open one wagon. And when the guards affirmed that those were the "Jews from Iași," she shouted back that "the Red Cross does not distinguish between those in need. If they are guilty, they would be brought to trial". Opening the wagon, the railway workers, and the sanitary workers remained speechless.

[Page 126]

In the words of our heroine, Viorica Agarici: "Then, I saw what kind of inferno it was there, in a layer of human waste and blood, tens and tens of people in each wagon, naked, maddened by thirst, packed like sardines, the dead, the dying and the living all together. For three days they were traveling in an unbearable heat, in freight cars hermetically sealed, which had been used before to transport carbide. The smell was unbearable".

"The shouts of Viorica Agarici were so loud, at the scene of these monstrosities, that the guards were intimidated, and they let the train being transferred to a garage line, where the orderlies took out tens of corpses, and those alive were showered with a hose. The wagons were later cleaned also, and those who remained alive were fed and allowed to drink, a most important thing, because they were condemned to death by thirst. A day and a night lasted this ordeal of bringing back to life those 1000 people who had remained alive in the train, and if they arrived at their destination, it was because of Viorica Agarici. Secretly, she gave them food and water supply, which enabled them to hold on till Călărași. And the colonel Anton Gherasim, at the order of the "general" that was Viorica Agarici, replaced the dirty straw in the wagons, with new dry straw. To what did Viorica expose herself – this small woman with a soul as big as a mountain?

Her deed could not remain without consequences, consequences worthy of those days. Some people walked for days in front of her house and her windows, placing flowers! Others, however, broke the windows and destroyed her house. And the lady had to resign from the Red Cross and flee to Bucharest. After the liberation, some of those saved by Victoria Agarici in 1941, have ensured for her a pension for 35 years, till her death in 1979. She did not have another pension. Others took care to lock Anton Gherasim in jail, as a war criminal, and confiscate his house. This is the way history is written!

[Page 127]

22 May 1983: On the *Avenue of the Righteous among People* in Jerusalem, in a special ceremony, her son, a man 75 years old, was invited to plant a tree in her memory, since she was included in the list of the "Righteous among People". It has been said there: "Viorica Agarici has rehabilitated the human race, demonstrating that although there are in the world beasts with the face of human beings, there are as well noble beings that deserve the biblical description of "creatures made in the shape and resemblance of God". But the old man (who had spent 17 years in prison as a son of an estate–owner) was not allowed to attend the ceremony. The tree was planted in his absence.

In place of conclusion

It was proposed that the street where Viorica has lived, and in the past was called Ion Agarici (now Ecaterina Teudoriu) receive back its past name in recognition of her heroism. Well deserved!

In 1937, I was the class delegate to the "Red Cross," the school delegate being prof. Iacob König, teacher of Latin, Romanian, French and German. The irony was that I was a Jew, but a delegate of the Red Cross, not the Red Star or the Red Crescent.

[Page 128]

We collected one Leu per pupil each month, and passed it to the teacher. We got a receipt! He and his son had been "travelers" in the train of death, where he was taken out convoluted around his son's neck, under the terrified eyes of Viorica Agarici, who had known him for many years. But his mouth, now closed, could not say to her anymore: "Be happy lady. None other than you believed in this principle: the Red Cross does not recognize country or nationality; it only recognizes the human being!"

In the avenue of the *Righteous among people*, in Jerusalem, the tree planted in 1983 grows along the others, carrying the inscription of one of those who proved by their lives and deeds that they are the real pillars that support humanity: Viorica Agarici, Lech Walesa, Helmut Kohl, have bent their heads as a sign of penitence for the happenings in their countries. Viorica Agarici has redeemed, we think, the evil deeds that happened in ours.

urns of vegetables, or whatever a man would sell, so that the monastery would have incense and candles".

(Bishop Melchisedek, *The Chronicles of Roman and the Bishopry of Roman*, vol. I, p. 330–331).

Appendix No. 3, 1742 Iaşi. Judgement Book given (by the Boyars of the Moldovian Divan) in the matter between the Jews Haim Lungu, Volia, and Haim and Isac, all from Roman, for an accounting of their partnership.

1742

"We inform you with this judgment book, as it came in front of the Divan of our Highness, our patron, his highness Ion Constantin Neculai, having in front of us these Jews, namely Haim Lungul and Volia, and another Haim and with Isac the son in law of Moisă, all from Roman and they complained in front of the Divan, saying that Haim Lungul and Volea and Haim, that they have suffered an injustice by Isac, because they were partners with Isac and another three Jews, namely with Haim Lungul and with Herscul and with another Isac this fall, and co-signed all four, on four quarters of paper, cut from the same sheet, so that they all be a fraternity and support each other no matter what happens. The signatures were given in the hand of Iancu the Jew to keep and now Isac. (…)

[Page 132]

(I.M.E.R., II/1, 1988, p. 158).

Appendix No. 4, 1743, February 11, Iaşi. Book of Judgements of the Moldovian Divan with respect to Pavăl the carter who claims that the Jew Cerbu from Roman should pay for a bull drowned in the Nistru River when he crossed it with a tank of wine from Movilău.

7251 (1753), February 11

Judgement granted to Cerbu the Jew from Roman, in the claim had with Pavăl the carter, Pavăl claiming from Cerbu the Jew a bull, alleging that he was in the service of the latter to transport a tank of wine from Movilău and as agreed to deliver it on the other side of the Nistru River. Once they arrived there, Cerbu directed him to cross the river at that location and when they were on the bridge it flooded and the bull drowned, and now he claims damages. Cerbu denied the allegations claiming that he had agreed with Pavăl to deliver the wine as directed and to pay him a fee for the service. It is acknowledged that nothing could have forced the carter to cross the bridge against his will. Thus Pavăl is instructed to leave Cerbu in peace and have the freedom to hold responsible the owner and attendant of the bridge, to pay for the bull, as it is customary."

(I.M.E.R. II/1, 1988, p.160)

[Page 133]

Appendix No. 5, 1756, July 12, Iaşi. Document written by the scribes about the debt between Jacob, a Jew from the town of Roman, and Ion from Iaşi, enforced by Constantin Mihail Cehan Racoviţă, the ruler.

We, Constantin Mihail Cehan Racoviţă prince and ruler of Moldova.

According to the decision of their highnesses boyars, in my realm, according to the right way and justice, I hereby seal with my seal the following:

Your Highness:

Under the authority vested in us by your order, appearing before us, was judged Jacob the Jew from the town of Roman, and Ion from here in Iaşi, and the following was found:

Jacob the Jew has shown in front of us two receipts from the year 7257 (?) which are written by Ion, first, that he took merchandise from Jacob for 156 lei and another receipt, that he owes another 300 lei, thus, for the two a total of 456 lei. Answered thus Jacob the Jew that for this money he pledged a certain shop, including the plot, in Târgul de Sus, and if he does not pay they will confiscate the shop. Now from these amounts they gave 60 lei and for the rest he is damaged, because he also pledged the shop in (...) places, taking out assurances on the old receipts. And for this Jacob the Jew is asking adjudication.

[Page 134]

Thus, confronting Ion and asking for his response to these debts, Ion did not deny the receipts, confessing that these are the debts, but claiming that when he inventoried the goods and placed the amounts in the receipts, he discovered that he was overcharged. Otherwise he claims that he paid some of the amounts of this debt, as it said on the copy of the receipt, which showed that the Jew's claims were lies. As for the overcharge, they are merely his sayings, because in seven years since these receipts were drafted he never said or complained about the calculations, how could he have suffered such a loss and never said anything?

Thus this is what we found in the way of our justice: Whereas the receipts of Jacob the Jew are good without any defects and whereas Ion rightfully owes the 465 lei we find that he is to pay this amount from which 60 lei is to be deducted as money that Jacob acknowledged to have received, thus leaving 396 and with this they will be even. As to the shop, since they held it as a pledge in three hands, the decision rests in your highnesses discretion. Since the receipts and calculations were signed by five merchants as witnesses and placed the receipts as pledges for the shop and in seven years they have said nothing it is recognized that they lack due diligence.

Sincerely your highnesses' servants.

[Page 135]

Let 7264. (?) 12th of July

I. Canta scribe, Raducanu Racovita Scribe
II. (U.M.E.R. II/2, 1990 p.21–22)

Appendix No. 6 1774 May–June (Moldova). Jews in the County of Roman

County of Roman
The Middle Assize

Jews

1. Iancul	2. Iosip	3. Leiba
4. Lehman	5. Leiba	6. Hercul
7. Marco	8. Berco	9. Haimu
10. Cerbul	11. Pascal	12. Nisin
13. Solomon		

(P.G. Dimitriev – *Moldova in feudal times, The Moldovian Censuses in the years 1772, 1773 and 1774*, vol. VII, part II. Chişinău, 1975)

Appendix No. 7 1790 July 20 / 1794 /, Moldova, Register arranged by Constantin Balş, major land owner and money lender regarding his debtors.

Register of money that is owed to me by some, with receipts and without receipts

1790 July 20 – (1794)

Lei	Bani no.	Roman County
500	2	Solomon son of Cerbea (or Cornea) Jew of Roman, 6 lei per bag monthly. With receipt dated 1790 April 29 and guarantors Bercu and Mindina, Jews of Trifeşti.

[Page 136]

Lei	Bani no.	Roman County
1000 (taken)	11	Lupul, Jew of Roman, 7 lei per bag monthly. With receipt dated 1790 March 1.
500	20	Leiba warden of Jews of Roman, 6 lei per bag monthly. With receipt dated 1787 October 1.
500	17	Bercu son of Leibu of Roman, 6 lei per bag monthly. With receipt dated 1786 January 22.
2500 (taken)	21	Lupul Jew Focsaneanu of Roman. But in 300 royal guilders, 1 guilder per hundred monthly and 1000 lei German currency. 5 lei per bag monthly. With receipt dated 1789 October 1.
350	22	Litman Jew of Roman 1 Leu per hundred monthly. With receipt =dated 1787 September 28.
300	24	Giacal Jew of Roman, from 10,12. With receipt dated 1787 October 9 and pawned the house he has in Roman next to Leibi's shop, his brother in law.
35,60 (given)	31	Peisală, the woman of Leibi of Roman, Iilosap Jew of Hălăuceşti. Receipt dated 1787 August 1 and Sain Jew of Roman guarantor and responsible of payment.
500	35	David son of Leibu of Roman, 6 lei per bag monthly. Receipt dated 1789 January 12.

[Page 137]

Lei	Bani no.	Roman County
400 taken	f.n.	Ioniţă Poghircu from Roman and Jewish butchers for 160 lambs which were sold, 2 lei each. Without receipt 1790 July 21.
848	36	Giacal Jew from Roman. With receipt dated 1790 July 19, for which they pawned some pearls and some big Guldens that Jewish women put on their heads. With interest from 10.12
5000 taken	f.n.	To Iosăpu Jew from Leşiache, who pawned 18 urns of horilcă, 1790 October 5.

Receipts that are for other obligations

Receipt 1 Pascal, grocer of Roman for 3 baskets of stones borrowed thereof 1790 April 25.

(I.M.E.R., 2 Feb, 1990 p. 348–350)

Appendix no. 8, 1790, August 20. Antoniu, Bishop of Roman, gave a plot of land for a house to the doctor Moise for definite settlement in town, deservingly "to one who served and continues to serve even now his house".

"We hereby inform you with this writing of our Bishopric that there exists here in the village of Roman a Jew named Moise with the profession of doctor and knowing him to be diligent and dedicated always at times of need, he would seek out the sick among the people of this domain and help them using his profession, from the time of our arrival here and until now, even before in the time of the deceased Bishop Ion, who was the bishop here, and we entrusted ourselves to the men of this house, who were in the same occupation and ready when they were called. And now since he is asking that we give him a plot for a house for his settlement in the town of Roman, we see one who served his fellows and continues to do so even though we paid for his travails, but since he was always diligent and dedicated to seek out the sick we give him the site for his house in front, and in length at the head of the main street toward the Precista Monastery on the western side, and he can establish his shop. That plot is for him to own and his descendants without anyone disturbing them , but he and his descendants will give every year as rent to the Bishopry, 4 vessels of wax, in consideration of which transaction we handed to him this our document signed by us with our own hands and sealed with the Bishopry seal.

[Page 138]

Antoniu, Bishop of Roman

(I.M.E.R. 2 Feb, 1990, p. 380–381)

Appendix no. 9 1794, Roman, The Jewish Artisan's Guild, decided to give the *Hevra Kadisha* [burial Society, lit. holy society], two lei every year.

"In Roman existed since 1794 a guild of artisans, probably an association (...) of various artisans. We find this in a note in the *Hevra Kadisha* code, which states: "It should be remembered that the "Poalei Tzedek" brotherhood indebted itself in front of the illustrious and Grand Rabbi from the capital Iaşi to give the Holy Society two lei annually".

[Page 139]

Note: At the given date, the **Dr. Iuliu Barasch Historic Society** kept a copy of the code.

(M. Schwartzfeld "The Age of the Jewish Existence in Moldova and Valachia" in "The Annals of the **Dr. Iuliu Barasch Historic Society**," year III, Bucharest, 1889, p. 132)

Appendix No. 10 1796, July 9 Roman. Constandin Olariul sold a house located in the Town of Roman next to the Jew Bercu's shop.

Whereas I Constandin Olariul form here in Roman, the son in law of Anuţa who was with Lupu Mămăligă, affirm with this act of mine that since I am in need of money, with the consent of my spouse Roxanda, and with the consent of my mother in law, I listed for sale the house given to me as dowry by my mother in law here in the town of Roman, in the back of the main street from the west, which house borders on top with the shop of Bercu the Jew and on the bottom with the shops of the Bishopry of Antonache Caramliu. And the site is bordered and marked by seven royal **stânjeni** [a measure of length], the width of the front on the west, and from there proceeds along both sides about 10 *stânjeni* in length and goes in an easterly direction toward the shops of the Bishopry, narrowing, and the back of the lot is only three *stânjeni* in width.

This house, after they called it for many days at auction, it came to be the price of seventy Lei, with which price I am satisfied, as well as my wife, and we both decided to give the house for this price, to whomever will take it. But the holy Bishopry of Roman, having a need of this house, they bid before any other buyer, because the shops of the Holy Bishopry are situated closer to this house. And they gave me all the money, in full in my hand, His Very Holy Father Veniamin Bishop of Roman, that is seventy Lei.

[Page 140]

Thus I, with this document of mine, I sold to the holy Bishopry this house with the plot that I described, to be owned by the holy Bishopry in peace without any disturbance neither from me, nor from my wife's family, nor from my wife. And in confirmation thereof we placed our name and fingerprint, me, my wife, my mother in law, my wife's sister and her husband. And it is also signed by other individuals who happened to witness this sale.

1796 July 9

From the Caretaker of Roman

The above named sellers appeared in front of us of their own will and sold the property, and are content with this price that came from the auction. This document is affirmed by us as well.

1796 July 12.

(I.M.E.R. II / 2, 1990, p. 435–436)

Appendix 11 April 20th, 1798 – June 22nd, 1802 (Miclăuşeni). Excerpts from the expenditure register of a glass factory from Miclăuşeni, Roman County, where the craftsman Avram worked and to which the tavern keeper Herşil supplied potash ashes.

Glass factory expenditure, April 20th, 1798

lei	bani
70	To Avram son of Iacob the craftsman, May 20th, 1789 with 14 lei me.
	For 100 merţi [plural form for mierţă = measure of capacity, 1 mierţă = aprox. 215 liters, RS]

[Page 141]

lei	bani
62	ashes at Verăşeni, inkeeper Herşil guarantor for the supervisor
70	Also to Jewish craftsman Avram son of Iacob August 12th, 1789, me. For 140 merţi of ashes at Tătăruşi through Herşil the innkeeper, 21 parale [para = currency unit] per mierţă, me.
14	Also to craftsman Avram son of Iacob, me. September 19th, 1789, when they got married.
21	Also to craftsman Avram son of Iacob the craftsman; October 13th, 1789, me.
70	To Avram son of Iacobu craftsman, also December 20th, 1798, me.
21	Also to Avram the craftsman, for 7 months for meat, the supervisor
35	To Avram son of Iacob craftsman, me March 21st, 1799
70	Also to Avram the craftsman, me June 5th, 1799
22	To Avram son of Iacob craftsman, October 5th, 1799 with three lei in debt
100	Also to Avram the craftsman, October 31st, 1799
20	Also to Avram the craftsman, December 15th, 1799
70	To Avram the craftsman; April 9th, 1800, to this day 80 galbeni [gold coins, RS] taken
23	To Avram the craftsman; June 4th, 1800
70	To Avram the craftsman July 16th, 1800, when they arrived from the furnace
70	To the craftsman as well; August 30th, 1800
70	To the craftsman as well; November 11th, 1800, taken
50	To the craftsman as well; December 28th, 1800
86	Corn to the storehouse for the servant craftsmen

[Page 142]

lei	bani
93	Wheat to the storehouse for the servant craftsmen
93	To the craftsman for meat
140	To the Jewish inkeeper craftsman; May 22nd, 1802
20	Three merți of bread also to him
20	His food

Note: The locality and the owner are not indicated in the register. The Miclăușeni estate was then owned by the Sturza family. C. Șerban shows that the work force in the glass factory was composed of skilled and unskilled workers; belonging to the first category was a foreign craftsman Avram son of Iacob. The collection of the ashes was done by the innkeeper Herșil. He collected the ashes from the distant villages: Verășani and Tătăruși.

(I.M.E.R. II/2, 1991 p. 445–447)

Appendix 12 May 27th, 1798, Iași. The Ruler of Moldova Alexandru Calimachi regulates the authority of the Bishop of Roman over the town and the town dwellers.

"For all wines and spirits sold in the public houses by Christian, Jewish or other town dwellers they will have to pay the bishopric two Bani [Romanian currency, 1/100 of a Leu] for each vadra [measure of capacity, approximately 3 gallons, RS] of wine sold in the pub, as well as one Ban for each oca [measure of capacity, about 1.2–1.5 liters, RS] of spirits; yet only the bishopric will be authorized to sell black oil [used to lubricate the wheels of the carts, RS]. Similarly, booth owners [in the market place, RS] will have to pay to the bishopric a leasing sum equal to one tenth of the rent received for the booth per annum; also each house owner dwelling on the municipal territory and its surroundings will give only one Leu and should be no more bothered; nor should the bishopric have any right to relocate the dwellers, i.e. to confiscate the lots from one person and give it to another, but everyone should own his lots, houses, selling booths and other dependencies, as they inherited from ancient times, from their grandparents and parents or bought from each other, so that the lot owners will only have to pay the lease for the lot as mentioned above."

(I.M.E.R. II/2, 1991 p. 452–453)

[Page 143]

Appendix 13 1820, Census of the Jews of Roman

120 tax payers, chartered Jews, but: 21 [of] status I, 37 status II, 46 status III.

Note: We find from a recent source the names of several of them. Izrail Haim, under Austrian protectorate, native of Cernăuţi, settled in the village of Chiliile, district of Roman and Bercu Haham. Of the 104 chartered Jews, 42 are under German and English protectorate and 16 are under Russian and French protectorate. (Stela Mărieş in *Studia et acta historiae iudaeroum Romaniae*, vol. I Bucureşti, 1996 p. 57–75 and Dumitru

Ivănescu in "S.A.H.I.R.", vol. II, Bucureşti, 1997, p. 62)

(State Archives Iaşi, Visteria Moldovei fund Tr. 166 inventory 184, register 9 files 245–264)

Appendix 14 1832, Statistics excerpt for the town of Roman

Mohorăni quarter; Jewish men 25, Jewish women 25, boys 32, girls 27, servants 12.

Târgul Vitelor quarter: Jewish men 77, Jewish women 83, boys 76, girls 77, male servants 20, female servants 6, their children 3, total 342.

[Page 144]

Uliţa quarter: Jewish men 146, Jewish women 158, boys 172, girls 157, male servants 38, female servants 20, total 691

Overall total: 1154

The document also mentions a synagogue (Jewish school)

(State Archives Iaşi, Visteria Moldovei, Tr. 644 inventory 708, reg. 77 files 3–4

Appendix 15 1843, Jewish merchants in Roman

Lot lease also from Jew Mihail son of Mititici – 45 lei

Lot lease also from Jew Israil son of Iţic – 60 lei

Lot lease also from Jew Naftule Kaufmann – 40 lei

Lease for other 4 booths from Haim Argintaru lei 400

Lease for another booth from David Argintaru lei 320

Lease for another booth from Iancu and Avram Jews lei 1400

("Parliamentary Annals of Romania", Vol. XII, part II, Bucureşti 1902 p. 532–534, 544)

Appendix 16 December 1844. Regarding the employment of Christian servants by Jews.

"To the honorable Council of this town Roman

The community of the town of Roman

One of the main concerns of the leadership overwhelmly was and still is that no Christian should serve the Jews, for which so many decisive injunctions are released from time to time.

[Page 145]

However, inspite all those [injunctions, RS], we find that not only are they not applied, but today to the contrary, almost all Jews have surrounded themselves with Christian servants of both sexes, to the measure that on one hand we have arrived to the situation that we cannot find servants for ourselves and on the other hand, what is more concerning is that such servants, and not at all a few in this town, are [getting] used to [serve] the Jews, disobeying the religion in which they were born and finding fit to abandon their moral and spiritual obligations to such extent that it is imosible to distinguish between some of them and the genuine Jews by their conduct, their speech or their customs. The consequences of that [situation] make us believe that in due time the Jews will succeed to bring such ignorant beings to the actual stampede of our predominant religion. They are imbued with such a damaging drive to extend the Jewish nation over the Christians without being even slightly stopped by the local authorities despite all the injunctions available to them for stopping such an evil. We the community, with all due respect, bring these to the knowledge of the Council and beg that our complaint be met with the adequate means in to bring about the necessary [steps] to eradicate this tendency forever".

(Gh. Ungureanu–Nic. Sendea –*Moldovan orders against the Jews*, vol. I up to 1880, Iași, 1942, p. 86–87)

Appendix 17 August 5th, 1852, The Council Report regarding the distance between churches and synagogues.

"The Department of Public Works, through report no. 3309, has submitted to the Council the complaint of the Roman Police Guard for the troubles caused by the Jewish synagogues, being established from time to time in the vicinity of the St. Neculai Church, by the conversion of dwellings to synagogues, without having first the permission of the authorities, and for the insupportable noise and shouting produced by the Jews inside and around those synagogues, especially at the time of the church service, causing scandal and considerable dissatisfaction to the Christians since the synagogue is no more distant than 24 stânjeni [measure of length] on one side and 45 stânjeni on the other side, and for this is required proper rectification. The Council, revising its account of the previous matters of the same kind, has decided that: Regarding the report no. 18.822 of 1837, on a synagogue being at a 37 stânjeni distance from the Church of St. Neculai in the town of Roman, granted the Jews the permission to use that school as a place of abode or to sell it to whomever they may find and establish it [the school/synagogue, RS] elsewhere".

[Page 146]

Appendix 18 1865–1866. The concern of the Roman Municipality with the building of the Jewish school.

The United Romanian Principalities March 18th, 1865

The Municipality of Urban Community Roman, N. 426

Gentlemen of the Jewish Community,

Taking into account that the existence of the Israelite schools in this town has not been regulated until now according to the directives of the Ministry of Religions, [they] will not be tolerated in the future and they are destined to be foreclosed – as well as regarding [your] proposal addressed to the Municipality that you have formed for the above mentioned

[Page 147]

purpose a committee composed of Messrs. Dr. Reitman, Iosub Catz, Leiba Focşăneanu, Nusen Schwartz, Aba Avram, Iţic Segal and Avram Cramer, who were assigned the duty to raise the budgetary means for establishing and maintaining one or more schools, according to the needs for the education of Israelite children, properly applied for and submitted to the Municipality.

Mayor (undersigned) Agarici

The United Romanian Principalities December 2nd, 1865

The Municipality of Urban Community Roman, N. 2929

Gentlemen Trustees,

Following the address received from Hon. District Prefect, N. 11.663, the undersigned is honored to invite you, in agreement with the Hon. Town Architect, to soon put together a plan for building a synagogue for worship and a school for education, which you will submit to the Municipality without delay for inspection and legalization according to the law.

Mayor (undersigned) Agarici

The United Romanian Principalities April 17th, 1866

The Municipality of Urban Community Roman, N. 1073

Gentlemen Trustees,

Considering that now the budget of the Religion has been regulated and a considerable sum was provided for the foundation of the school for education, the undersigned honorably invites you to immediately regulate its foundation, since as you have been informed, the Municipality can no more tolerate that the education of the children of the Israelite religion, should be to this day, outside the prescription of the law for public education in any form.

[Page 148]

Mayor (undersigned) Agarici

The Municipality of Urban Community Roman, July 4th, 1866

N. 1899

Gentlemen Trustees,

To your address no. 78, the undersigned responds that the foundation of a school for the education of children being an imperative necessity for any religion, you should therefore take pain by all means to purchase the required lot urgently. Consequently you have the right for the good and the prosperity of that religion to get in touch [with the sellers] for the purchase of the proposed building, which may facilitate the worship and the education of the children. The result is expected from you without delay.

Mayor (undersigned) illegible

(Suchard Rivenzon – *The Jewish School in the Town of Roman*, Roman, Beram the father Publishing, 1933, p. 16–17)

[Page 149]

Appendix no. 19 The Statistics of the Roman County Jews, 1898

Bara, small town, 407 inhabitants, almost all Jews

Bozieni, small town, 1000 inhabitants, most of them Jews

Bozieni, village, 1 Jewish family

Brănişteni de jos, village, 2 Jewish families

Brăteşti, village, idem

Brătuleşti, village, idem

Broşteni, rural community, 1 Jewish family

Buciumi, village, 3 Jewish families

Butnăreşti, village, 5 Jewish families

Cordunul, community, 1 Jewish family

Criveşti, village, 5 Jewish families

Dagăta, village, 2 Jewish families

Dămieneşti, rural community, 47 Jewish families

Dămieneşti, small town, 45 Jewish families

Drăgeşti, village, 9 Jews

Fundul, district, 201 Jewish families, in 67 villages and 2 small towns: Băceşti and Dămieneşti

Galbeni, rural community, 7 Jewish families

Galbeni, village, 6 Jewish families

Hălăuceşti, rural community, 15 Jewish families

Miclauşeni, rural community, 11 Jewish families

Mogoşeşti, rural community, 17 Jewish familiesv

[Page 150]

Mogoşeşti, village, 2 Jewish families

Moldova, district, 81 Jewish families

Muscelul de sus, village, 15 Jewish families

Roman, city, 13,334 inhabitants: Romanians, Jews, Armenians, Hungarians, Greeks, Germans

Săbăoani, rural community, 10 Jewish families

(I. Lahovary *The Big Geographic Dictionary of Romania*, Bucharest, 1898, vol. I–IV)

Appendix No. 20 the Statistics of the Jews in the beginning of the 20th century, Roman county

Plasa Fundu [The Fundu District]

Avereşti, 1,446 inhabitants, 5 Jews

Băceşti, 1,958 inhabitants, 526 Jews

Băluşeşti, 1,292 inhabitants, 13 Jews

Bătrâneşti, 865 inhabitants, 6 Jewsv

Bozieni, 1,957 inhabitants, 13 Jews

Brăteşti, 1,249 inhabitants, 7 Jews

Chiliile, 1,602 inhabitants, 36 Jews

Ciutureşti, 1,043 inhabitants, 16 Jews

Dămieneşti , 1,260 inhabitants, 194 Jews

Giurgeni, 1,742 inhabitants, 10 Jews

Iucşeşti, 872 inhabitants, 1 Jew

Negri, 1,329 inhabitants, 16 Jews

Oniceni, 861 inhabitants, 22 Jews

Roşiori, 1,141 inhabitants, 2 Jews

Plasa Siretu de sus [Upper Siret District]

Băra, 2057 inhabitants, 308 Jews

Boghicea, 2,525 inhabitants, 20 Jews

Dagăţa, 2,541 inhabitants, 16 Jews

Gădinţi, 1,068 inhabitants, 4 Jews

Heleştieni, 2,438 inhabitants, 6 Jews

[Page 151]

Miclăuşeni, 3,424 inhabitants, 19 Jews

Păncești, 2,118 inhabitants, 15 Jews

Sagna, 2,226 inhabitants, 29 Jews

Scheia, 1,735 inhabitants, 26 Jews

Stăniţa, 2,728 inhabitants, 26 Jews

Strunga, 2,241 inhabitants, 26 Jews

Plasa Moldova

Bahna, 1,615 inhabitants, 21 Jews

Bărjoveni, 716 inhabitants, 4 Jews

Bogzești, 1,515 inhabitants, 11 Jews

Botești, 1,751 inhabitants, 9 Jews

Broșteni, 765 inhabitants, 12 Jews

Cârligi, 2,211 inhabitants, 28 Jews

Cordunu, 1,531 inhabitants, 15 Jews

Dulcești, 1,326 inhabitants, 48 Jews

Elizabeta Doamna, 1,479 inhabitants, 32 Jews

Galbeni, 1,211 inhabitants, 59 Jews

Gherăești, 2,169 inhabitants, 5 Jews

Hălăucești, 2,421 inhabitants, 40 Jews

Mircești, 1,560 inhabitants, 8 Jews

Mogoșești, 2,198 inhabitants, 51 Jews

Pildești, 1,043 inhabitants, 3 Jews

Onișcani, 874 inhabitants, 44 Jews

Porcești, 1,643 inhabitants, 19 Jews

Roman, 16,228 inhabitants, 6,432 Jews

Săbăconi, 3,039 inhabitants, 6 Jews

Secuieni, 1,250 inhabitants, 1 Jew

Tămășeni, 1,114 inhabitants, 2 Jews

Trifești, 2,133 inhabitants, 10 Jews

Tupulaţi, 1,155 inhabitants, 14 Jews

Văleni, 1,800 inhabitants, 4 Jews

(Leonida Colescu *General Census of the Romanian Population, Bucharest,* 1905)

[Page 152]

Appendix No. 21 1929, Census of Jewish Population – Excerpts

Koffler Mendel, pharmacist, born in Roman, age 47

Kivilevici Marcu, cantor, born in Bălţi, settled in Roman in 1920

Koenig Iacob, professor, age 40 , born in Russia (Moldaviţa), settled in Roman in 1923

Margulius Aron, age 60, soap factory

Marcovici Silvian, age 34, knitwear factory

Moscovici Bercu, age 29, journalist, born in Piatra Neamţ, wife Cerna, born in Lemberg

Moldoveanu Gherş, school teacher, born in Bălţi, settled in 1919 in Roman, age 36

Moscovici Leon, dentist, born in Roman, age 27, wife Mina, dentist, age 22

Marc Bucă, age38, industrialist, born in Roman

Mendrochowitz Alfred, age 31, physician, born in Roman

Meyr David, age 39, dentist, born in Chişinău

Neuman Iosef, age 49, professor, born in Botoşani

Popydodi Ignat, age 42, musician, born in Kiev

Pascal Iancu, age 60, messenger, born in Roman

Rozenthal Solomon, age 46, photographer, born in Iaşi

Rosenberg Moise, manufacturer, born in Bacău

Rubin Lippa, age 44, Rabbi, born in Poland and settled in Roman in 1909

Rosen Sigmund, age 48, manufacturer, born in Roman

Rivensohn Suchard, age 40, the Director of the Hebrew–Romanian schools of Roman, wife Clara, age 31, sons ElisÃ©e and Abraham

Rozenberg Mendel, age 45, born in Bacău, manufacturer

[Page 153]

Renţler Aron, age 36, born in Roman, manufacturer

Seider Nathan, age 45, born in Fălticeni, manufacturer

Strul Leib, age 42, cantor, born in Maramureş

Sendel Iancu, age 65, born in Iţcani–Suceava, settled in Roman in 1925

Somer Nathan, age 22, journalist, born in Roman

Şor Zalman, age 22, pharmacist, born in Roman, son of Mendel, shoemaker

Schor Maximilian, age 35, attorney, born in Roman

Stein Leon, age 50, bank manager, born in Roman

Stein Iosif, age 30, manufacturer, born in Roman

Schachter Zalman, age 45, ritual slaughterer, born in Vatra–Dornei, settled in Roman in 1926

Schwartz Suchăr, age 29, photographer, born in Huşi

Schweitzer Bercu, age 31, typographer, born in Roman

Schor Albert, age 33, manufacturer, born in Roman

Schachter Moses, age 52, manufacturer, born in Boian–Bucovina

Trister Israel, age 29, M. D., born in Ploieştiv Wacher Ioseph, age 51, M. D., born in Siret

Werner Solomon, age 50, manufacturer and merchant, born in Botoşani, settled in Roman in 1899

Welt Iancu, age 60, assistant surgeon, born in Roman

Wechsler Avram, age 48, physician, born in Botoşani, settled in Roman in 1907

Wolfsohn Zigmund, age 53, cantor, born in Tg. Frumos, settled in Roman in 1907

Zingher Mauriciu, age 30, attorney, born in Roman

[Page 154]

(406   Jewish   families   of   1645   souls)
(A.S.N.F.C.E.R., Register 1/1929 – Census of the Jewish population in Roman

Appendix No. 22 1938 Statistics of the Jewish population in Roman

Excerpts, letters I–L

Ioseph Abraham, born in Roman in 1904, physician, wife Hana, school teacher, born in 1907

Isacsohn Iosub, born in Roman, 1902, Rabbi

Isacsohn Solomon, born in Mihăileni in 1872, Rabbi of the Jewish communities from 1907

Katz Riven, born in Hangu–Neamţ, in 1894, ritual slaughterer

Konig Iacob, born in 1890, professor

Leivandman Heindl, born in Mihăileni, in 1885, ritual slaughterer

Lazarovici Ioil, born in Iaşi, in 1863, owner of a cinema hallv Leiba Moise, born in Roman, in 1907, physician

Leibovici Jean, born in Dămieneşti–Roman, in 1903

Leibovici Lia, born in Iaşi, in 1911, chemist

Leizer Bercu, born in Roman, in 1903, physician

Leizerovici Iosub, born in Roman, in 1901, manufacturer

(A.S.N.F.C.E.R., Census of the Jewish population in Roman 1938, letters I–L)

Appendix No. 23 Jews evacuated from villages and towns, November 1940

Sufrin Simcha, evacuated from Tg. Băceşti to Roman, merchant, claims losses of 2 million Lei, due to real–estate sold under the racist laws regime, and fear of total loss by confiscation by the C.N.R. Grocery and smithy merchandise were lost or destroyed.

Haim D. Faibiş, evacuated from rural community Băceşti to Roman, age 40, then evacuated to Tg. Jiu, claims losses of 675,000 Lei.

Leibovici Benţin, evacuated from rural community Băceşti to Tg. Jiu, with his wife and child, claims losses of 8 million Lei.

Şarf Maria, age 54, housewife, evacuated from rural community Băceşti to Roman, claims losses of 2 million Lei.

Haimovici Raşela, age 58, previously the owner of a warehouse of yeast and fish, evacuated from rural community Băceşti to Roman, claims losses of 500,000 Lei.

Faibiş Herşcu, age 49, previously the owner of a soda factory since 1923, evacuated to Tg. Jiu, claims losses of 1,872,390 Lei.

Faibiş Iosub D. Faibiş, age 43, merchant, evacuated from rural community Băceşti to Tg. Jiu, claims losses of 1,670,000 Lei.

Sainfeld H. Clara, age 46, owned a yard–goods shop, evacuated from rural community Băceşti to Roman, claims losses of 1,200,000 Lei.

Rebeca Veis, evacuated from her building in rural community Băceşti to Roman, claims losses of 2,200,000 Lei.

Iosef Iosef, age 54, evacuated from rural community Dămieneşti to Tg. Jiu, claims losses of 500,000 Lei.

Brucăr Smil, age 34, merchant in rural community Dămieneşti, evacuated to Tg. Jiu.

[Page 155]

[Page 156]

Leibovici Iosub of rural community Dămieneşti, grocery and crockery merchant, evacuated to Tg. Jiu, claims losses of 800,000 Lei.

Rosenfeld Iancu, from rural community Dămieneşti, age 61, evacuated to Tg. Jiu.

Rothenberg Iţic, from rural community Dămieneşti, age 51, evacuated to Tg. Jiu; grocery and textile merchant and cereals warehouse, claims losses of 3500000 Lei.

Leiba Leizer, merchant from rural community Dămieneşti, evacuated to Roman, claims losses of 800,000 Lei.

David Leiba a.k.a. Leon Segal, from rural community Dămieneşti, age 48, evacuated to Tg. Jiu, his family evacuated to Roman, claims losses of 450,000 Lei.

Rotenberg Şloim, merchant from rural community Dămieneşti, age 60, evacuated to Tg. Jiu, claims losses of 1,500,000 Lei.

Rotenberg Herşcu, merchant from rural community Dămieneşti, age 60, evacuated to Tg. Jiu with a child, claims losses of 1,178,000 Lei.

Fruchtman Iancu, merchant from rural community Dămieneşti, age 60, evacuated to Roman, claims losses of 3,900,000 Lei.

Herşcu Moise, shoemaker, from rural community Dămieneşti, age 61, evacuated to Tg. Jiu, then to Celar and Radomir.

Şmil Marcu, from rural community Dămieneşti, merchant, age 30, evacuated to Roman, claims losses of 1 million Lei.

Iosub Marcu, from rural community Dămieneşti, shoemaker, age 39, evacuated to Roman, claims losses of 400,000 Lei.

Şmil Ghidale, from rural community Dămieneşti, tailor, age 51, evacuated to Tg. Jiu, then to Celar and Radomir.

[Page 157]

Sura Bandel, merchant, age 52, evacuated from Bozieni–Balş to Roman, claims losses of 1.5 million Lei.

Catz Leizer, grains merchant, age 66, evacuated from Bozieni–Balş to Roman, claims losses of 1 million Lei.

Lupu Aron, grains merchant, age 38, evacuated from Bozieni–Balş to Roman.

Beiniş Soifer, store keeper, evacuated from Bozieni–Balş to Roman, claims losses of 3 million Lei.

Solomon Haim and Leia, ages 48 and 44 respectively, owners of a grocery and a grains warehouse, evacuated from Bozieni–Balş to Roman, claims losses of

3.5 million Lei.

Nehume Haia, housewife from Bâra, evacuated to Roman, claims losses of 2.5 million Lei.

Vigder Froim, age 42, grocery and textiles merchant, evacuated to Tg. Jiu, claims losses of 2,225,000 Lei.

Hudea L. Moise, age 50, merchant from Bâra, evacuated to Tg. Jiu, claims losses of 5.5 million Lei.

Iliescu Strul, age 35, merchant from Bâra, evacuated to Tg. Jiu, then to Caracal, claims losses of 3.5 million Lei.

Hudea F. Moise, farmer, estate owner from Bâra, age 50, evacuated to Tg. Jiu, then to Caracal and Roman. Claims the following losses: 2 houses, barns, farm, agriculture inventory, livestock, apiary, of which: houses worth of 2 million Lei, barns worth 2 million Lei, farm house 500,000 Lei, agriculture inventory 1.5 million Lei, livestock (cattle, horses) worth

[Page 158]

6.5 million Lei, apiary worth of 650,000 Lei, clothes, shoes, lingerie worth of 1.6 million Lei. A total of 26,750,000 Lei.

Leibovici Rata, age 54, tobacco warehouse in Bâra, evacuated to Roman, claims losses of 1.8 million Lei (house, warehouse, stable, farm)

Hudea Solomon, age 45, merchant from Bâra, evacuated to Tg. Jiu, returned to Roman after 3 months.

Cahan Iosub, age 60, merchant from Bâra, evacuated to Tg. Jiu.

Gabor Betty, paints shop from Bâra, age 56, evacuated to Roman, claims losses of 1.5 million Lei.

Enciu Herşcu, merchant from Elizabeta Doamna, age 38, evacuated to Roman, claims losses of 1.5 million Lei.

The Jewish community of Bâra has suffered losses of 16 million Lei, that of Dămieneşti losses of 18 million, that of Băceşti 50 million, and that of Bozieni–Balş 8 million Lei.

Ghidale Bercu, merchant from Cuza Vodă, age 50, evacuated to Tg. Jiu.

Pascal Zisu, merchant from the village Dobânda, com. Doljeşti, age 47, evacuated to Tg. Jiu.

Faer Iuda, owner of a grocery store and a pub, from the village Vulpăşeşti, com. Sagna, evacuated to Tg. Jiu.

Leiba Iancu, merchant from the village of Davideni, com. Păstrăveni, age 65, evacuated to Roman, claims losses of 10 million Lei.

Iancu Moisă, shop owner from com. Gădinţi, age 45, evacuated to Tg. Jiu, claims losses of 350,000 Lei.

[Page 159]

Bercovici Iterman, merchant from Călugăreni, age 44, evacuated to Tg. Jiu, claims losses of 2.5 million Lei.

Bercu Raşela, owner of a shop and a distillery in com. Budeşti–Ghica, evacuated to Roman, claims losses of 1.2 million Lei.

Moisă Herşcu Liza, from com. Budeşti–Ghica, age 60, owner of a pub, claims losses of 1 million Lei.

Cramer Marcu, merchant from com. Icuşeşti, age 45, evacuated to Tg. Jiu, claims losses of 700,000 Lei.

Lupu Burăh, merchant from com. Brătianu, evacuated to Roman, claims losses of 770,000 Lei.

Dolheşteanu Fany, owner of a shop and pub in Boteşti, age 52, evacuated to Roman.

Leizerovi Iancu, from Roman, age 39, commerce of grains, grocery and drinks, claims losses of 8 million Lei (house, business, merchandise).

Schwartz Suchăr, photographer in Roman; in 1941 his photo studio at Ştefan cel Mare St. was destroyed at the order of the mayor and at the advice of the sanitary services of the city of Roman; claims losses of 1.4 million Lei.

Avramescu Aurel, photographer in Roman, idem.

Iuster Filip, attorney in Roman, evacuated to Tg. Jiu on 22 Jun 1941, and on 5 Sep 1942 to Transnistria. On 20 Mar 1944 he was arrested and sent to the concentration camp in Moineşti. As he was arrested, the secret service confiscated his clothes, lingerie and shoes at the worth of 1 million Lei. When he was deported to Transnistria, they confiscated his house, worth 500,000 Lei.

[Page 160]

David Iosub, from Roman, merchant; his building, worth 5.5 million Lei was destroyed.

Velt Solomon, merchant in Roman, age 37, claims losses of 6 million Lei (pub and barn).

Nusim David, owned a notions and accessories store in Roman, evacuated to Tg. Jiu, claims losses of 3 million Lei.

Lupu Smil, from Urecheni – Neamţ, merchant, 67 years old, evacuated to Roman, claims losses of 1.2 million Lei.

Gluckman Aron, a traveling salesman from Băceşti, age 45, evacuated to Tg.

Jiu, claims losses of 400,000 Lei.

Vaintraub David, Hebrew teacher, from rural community Băceşti, age 65, claims losses of 1.5 million Lei.

Rottman Moise, baker from rural community Băceşti, age 42, evacuated to Tg. Jiu.

Weisman Abel, from rural community Băceşti, age 65, textile merchant, bookshop, haberdashery and newspapers, evacuated to Tg. Jiu, claims losses of 6.5 million Lei.

Davidovici Iosif, commercial clerk from rural community Băceşti, age 31, evacuated to Tg. Jiu accused of Zionist propaganda, claims losses of 2.5 million Lei.

Cupferman Mendel David, merchant from rural community Băceşti, age 51, evacuated to Tg. Jiu, then to Caracal, returned to Roman in Nov. 1941, claims losses of 4 million Lei.

Mark Mendel, rabbi and ritual slaughterer in Băceşti, age 56, evacuated to Caracal and Tg. Jiu.

Cojocaru Şloim, innkeeper and wine warehouse from rural community Băceşti, evacuated to Roman, claims losses of 10 million Lei.

[Page 161]

Iosepovici Iosef, textile merchant, from Băceşti, age 46, evacuated to Tg. Jiu, claims losses of 9.5 million Lei.

Schönfeld Leiba, merchant from Tg. Băceşti, age 63, evacuated to Tg. Jiu, claims losses of 14 million Lei.

Cojocaru Moisă Marcu, a.k.a. Marcovici, from rural community Băceşti, wood, iron, and construction ware merchant, evacuated to Tg. Jiu, claims losses of 1.8 million Lei.

Ruhla David Moisă, age 55, from rural community Băceşti, merchant of grocery, iron, haberdashery and crockery, evacuated to Roman, claims losses of 6 million Lei.

Rosenstein Mendel, age 58, from rural community Băceşti, commerce and factory (crockery).

Herman Aron, age 48, from rural community Băceşti, evacuated to Tg. Jiu and Caracal, claims losses of 1.8 million Lei.

Marcusohn Zalman, age 41, from rural community Băceşti, merchant, evacuated to Tg. Jiu.

Crainăr Manoilă, age 59, from rural community Băceşti, Hebrew teacher, evacuated to Tg. Jiu.

Abramovici Iţic, age 43, expeditor at the railway station at rural community Băceşti, evacuated to Tg. Jiu.

Abramovici Solomon, age 70, from rural community Băceşti, forest exploiter, claims losses of 800,000 Lei.

Schwartz Bercu, age 39, from rural community Băceşti, shoes and haberdashery merchant, evacuated to Tg. Jiu, claims losses of 5 million Lei.

Zucker Toivy, age 60, butcher from Tg. Băceşti, evacuated to Tg. Jiu and Caracal, returned 4 Nov 1941.

[Page 162]

Herşcovici Iţic, age 36, from rural community Băceşti, merchant, evacuated to Tg. Jiu, claims losses of 2.5 million Lei.

Vigder Litman Herşcu, age 61, from rural community Băceşti, merchant, evacuated to Tg. Jiu, claims losses of 4 million Lei.

Velt Zeilig, age 53, from rural community Băceşti, merchant, evacuated, claims losses of 29.5 million Lei, consisting of 2 buildings, barns, farm, and merchandise.

Lewensohn Strul, age 50, from rural community Băceşti, textile merchant, evacuated to Tg. Jiu and Caracal, returned at 4 Nov 1941, claims losses of 6 million Lei.

Mendel L. Mendel, age 60, from rural community Băceşti, textile merchant, claims losses of 4,598,000 Lei.

Braunstein Leiba, age 40, from rural community Băceşti, store owner and transport, evacuated to Tg. Jiu, claims losses of 3 million Lei.

Cojocaru Moise, age 49, merchant in rural community Băceşti, evacuated to Tg. Jiu, claims losses of 3 million Lei.

Croitor a.k.a Grimberg Sulim Moisă, age 50, from rural community Băceşti, bootmaker, evacuated to Tg. Jiu and Caracal, returned to Roman on 4 Sep 1942.

Herşcu Toivi, age 60, bootmaker from rural community Băceşti, evacuated to Tg. Jiu.

Crai Burăh, age 56, merchant from rural community Băceşti , evacuated to Tg. Jiu.

Cojocaru Moisă Marcu, age 45, wood expeditor from rural community Băceşti, evacuated to Tg. Jiu.

[Page 163]

Haimovici Hascal, age 48, merchant from rural community Băceşti, evacuated to Tg. Jiu and Caracal, returned to Roman, claims losses of 3.1

million Lei.

Segal Şulăm, age 46, tinsmith from rural community Băceşti, evacuated to Tg. Jiu, returned September 1941.

Cojocaru Chisiel, age 45, innkeeper from rural community Băceşti, evacuated to Tg. Jiu and Caracal.

Stoleru Zalman, bootmaker from rural community Băceşti, evacuated to Tg. Jiu.

Abramovici Herşcu, age 29, clerk from rural community Băceşti, evacuated to Tg. Jiu and Caracal.

Iancu Enghel, age 41, forests clerk from rural community Băceşti, evacuated to Tg. Jiu.

Moscovici Beniamin, age 52, bootmaker from rural community Băceşti, evacuated to Tg. Jiu and Caracal.

Moisă Ghelberg, age 44, merchant from rural community Băceşti, evacuated to Tg. Jiu.

Zilberman Avram, age 44, harness merchant from rural community Băceşti, evacuated to Tg. Jiu, claims losses of 1.3 million Lei.

Weinberg David, age 69, from rural community Băceşti, formerly factory owner, owner of lime and cement warehouse, evacuated to Tg. Jiu and Caracal, claims losses of 4.6 million Lei.

Lazarovici Marx, age 50, merchant from rural community Băceşti, evacuated to Tg. Jiu, Craiova, and Caracal, claims losses of 5 million Lei.

Kern Leizer, age 47, grains commerce from rural community Băceşti, evacuated to Tg. Jiu and Caracal.

David B. Pincu, age 47, merchant from rural community Băceşti, evacuated to Tg. Jiu.

[Page 164]

Cojocaru S. Kisiel, age 35, furrier from rural community Băceşti, evacuated to Tg. Jiu and Caracal.

Rothenberg Haim Hascal, age 61, merchant in Băceşti, evacuated to Tg. Jiu, returned in September 1941.

Benis Noe, age 35, merchant and book keeper from rural community Băceşti, evacuated to Tg. Jiu and Caracal, returned to Roman, claims losses of 3 million Lei.

Cohn Iţic Aron, age 51, textile and haberdashery merchant from rural community Băceşti, evacuated to Tg. Jiu and Caracal, returned in September 1941.

(A.S.N.F.C.E.R. individual questionnaire of the Jews evacuated from villages, small towns and cities, excerpts, Reg. 103/1945, 104/1945)

Note: In July 1941, there were in Roman 670 Jews evacuated from villages and small towns. We do not know exactly how many of them were suspected of communism and evacuated to Tg. Jiu,

Of the 3 researched registers, containing a number of 103 Jews evacuated from towns and villages, 67 were sent to Tg. Jiu.

Of those suspected of communism, the composition is as following:

– merchants 48
– small industry 1
– clerks 3
– intellectuals 3
– craftsmen (shoemakers, tailors, tinsmiths, owners of workshops) 12
– 1 estate owner

[Page 165]

Appendix 24 Jan 7th – Apr 3rd, 1941. The City of Roman Police reports to the Police Inspectorate Iaşi regarding the state of mind of the Jewish population of Roman, towards the beginning of the war.

Roman City Police (Jan 15th, 1941)
"In response to your order No. 117 of January 7th, 1941, we report that in our precinct the Jewish Community collects money for helping the poor, for the maintenance of the schools and for the Jewish hospital. No connection of the existing aid committees with overseas could be established."

Roman City Police (Jan 29th, 1941)
"In response to your order No. 23.793 of September 23rd, 1940 repeated with No. 117 of January 7th, 1941, we report that in this Police Precinct the communities do have aid committees for social welfare and for culture, but only as provided by the statutes and the regulations of October 12th, 1936. From investigation made among those, we did not obtain any affirmative information that any new such committees have been set up after the detrimental notice given by the Ministry of the Interior in 1940, or that they receive aid from abroad."

Roman City Police (April 3rd, 1941)

"In response to your order No. 7147–S of March 24th, c.y., we have the honor to report that from the investigation made within the perimeter of this precinct, we found no evidence regarding the proposals *made to the Jewish leaders in Romania by English envoys*. The matter remains under scrutiny".

[Page 166]

Note: Hence, two and a half months before the beginning of the war the Jews were suspected of collaboration with the English not the Russians! (I. Ludo – *LBy Whose Order?* Bucharest, 1947, Răspântia Publishing House p. 37, 50)

Appendix 25 Documents from the archives in Roman, related to the pogrom in Iaşi.

Official Report No.8

Today, June 25th, 1941, the undersigned Z. Goldenstein, president of the burial society of the Jewish Community in Roman, received 64 Jewish residents sent by the Community for digging, according to the order given by the Municipality of Roman. All of them, according to the drawn up list, worked at the cemetery until 6 pm, with a two–hour lunch intermission.

Signature

Z. Goldenstein

Official Report No. 9

[I,] the undersigned Z. Goldenstein, continued today the digging at the cemetery with the same number of people as yesterday, namely 64, the work being performed according to the order given by the honored Municipality of Roman.

June 26th, 1941

Z. Goldenstein

Official Report No. 10

Today, June 27th 1941, the undersigned Z. Goldenstein, mandatory guardian of the Jewish Communities of Roman, continued the works at the cemetery, with the number of 64 people sent by the Community, according to the order given by the honored Municipality of Roman, working without intermission, with short rests until 12 o'clock, restarting work at 2 pm, until 6 pm.

Z. Goldenstein

[Page 167]

Official Report No. 11

Today, Sunday June 29th, while at the cemetery for regular inspection, I found out the water from the Moldova [River, RS] was constantly breaking down parts of the river bank making it necessary to take measures for the safety of the cemetery. At the same time I took possession of the new gate towards the Valter factory, the personnel on duty being there. I gave some orders for the internal service and left the cemetery at 5 pm.

Z. Goldenstein

Official report No. 12

Today, Friday July 4th, 1941, arriving at the cemetery for regular inspection, the guard Petre Câmpeanu gave [me] the following account:

During the night of July 3–4, about one to half past one, after midnight, he was awakened by the authorities and advised to remain awake as they are bringing in some wounded.

After about a couple of hours, namely at three–three thirty a lorry arrived of which a number of 38 corpses was unloaded and were buried in a common grave of those dug according to the orders of the honored Municipality of Roman. About 7 am, 9 more dead were brought in, which were buried in a common grave adjacent to the former one. Then, at eleven–eleven thirty another 6 dead were brought in, being buried in the same grave with the 9 of the morning.

[Page 168]

From the information obtained as well as from the declarations made by those who brought in the above mentioned dead, they originate from the trains with Jews evacuated from Iaşi and had deceased for various reasons.

Z. Goldenstein

J. Leizerovici

I attest the above

The guard of the Jewish cemetery of Roman

Official Report No. 28

The work by Jewish hands at the cemetery within the frame of the work for community benefit ended on July 31st, 1941 – following the categorical orders received from the commander of the Roman Recruiting Center, which stopped summoning people for work without the direct order of the Army Supreme Headquarters.

Between July 25th and July 31st, 1941 the following were carried out within the frame of this work:

A number of 6 common graves dug by the orders of the honored Municipality, M.O.N.T. service.

A stone paved road from the side gate of the cemetery to the common graves, conforming to the order of the same service.

Clearing of weeds as much as possible and paving with pebbles the main alleys and the old cemetery up to the Rabbis' chapel.

Lifting and ordering the bricks of that part of the fence destroyed by the earthquake of November 1940.

Strengthening and disinfecting the common graves to prevent severe trouble.

[Page 169]

Clearing all the pathways and alleys of fallen tombstones and scattered bricks. (...) Today, the wooden fence of the two common graves of Iaşi residents dead in known circumstances was completed. (...)

Z. Goldenstein J. Leizerovici

Official Report No. 31

Today, August 31st, 1941, in the presence of Mr. Berthold Rohrlich, the president of the Community, Iulius Istein vice president, the guardians of the cemetery section and a very small number of leading figures of the Jewish Community of Roman, Rabbi Mendel Frenkel, the rabbi of the Jewish Community, assisted by Cantor T. Wolfsohn officiated a moving divine service for the rest of the souls of the 53 Iaşi residents which an inexorable fate has sent to find anonimous graves in our cemetery. No related speech was made. (...)

Z. Goldenstein J. Leizerovici

(A.S.N.F.C.E.R., Dossier 33 (Register of cemetery inspections / 1941–1942)

Appendix No. 26, July 2nd, 1941. Jews from the death trains deceased and buried within the territory of the former District of Roman.

a.

Official Report

We, Second Lieutenant Triandaf Aurel from the mobile Gendarmes Legion Iaşi, together with Second Lieutenant Popescu D. of Police Company No. 60 Roman, attest that a number of 327 (three hundred and twenty seven) bodies were unloaded from the train of Jews at the Mirceşti train station, and

[Page 170]

were buried at the outskirts of the village Iugani – Roman.

For which we have drawn the present official report.

SLt. Res.(signature) Triandaf Aurel SLt. (signature) Popescu

b.

Secret

No. 37955/July 9th

Gendarmes Legion Roman

To

General Inspectorate of the Gendarmerie

Gendarmerie Service

I have to report the following:

On July 2nd, this year, conforming to the order of the Grand General Quarters, a number of 386 Jews, men of all ages, brought by the train from Iaşi in closed wagons, were buried on the Siret river meadow in the Mirceşti – Roman village. During the day of July 2nd, 1941, anumber of 172 Jews dead in the wagons of the train that transported Jews evacuated from the city of Iaşi were buried within the territory of the village of Săbăoani.

Gendarmes Legion Commander

Major (signature) N. Ştefanescu

(a.–"R.C.M." 773 / January 1994, b. *Martyrdom of the Jews of Romania*, Bucharest. 1991, p. 115)

c. Jews from Iaşi from the death trains deceased within the territory of the former District of Roman.

Leib Iţic from Iaşi, builder – village Mirceşti–Roman

Lupu Saraga from Iaşi, grinder – village Mirceşti–Roman

[Page 171]

Teitel Iosef from Iaşi, laborer – village Mirceşti–Roman

Vigder Volf Neamtzu, Iaşi, waiter – village Mirceşti–Roman

Sami Vigder Neamtzu, Iaşi, waiter – village Mirceşti–Roman

Iancu Zinger, Iaşi – village Mirceşti–Roman

Moise Iosef Ulner, Iaşi, merchant – village Mirceşti–Roman

Moise Smilovici, Iaşi, printer – village Mirceşti–Roman

Bercu Meer, Iaşi, leather dresser, – village Mirceşti–Roman

Strul Moscovici, Vaslui, carpenter – village Mirceşti–Roman

Iancu Bărbuţă, Iaşi – village Mirceşti–Roman

Pincas Sloim Smilovici, Iaşi – village Mirceşti–Roman

Iţic Smilovici, Iaşi – village Mirceşti–Roman

Friederich Schwartz, Iaşi – village Mirceşti–Roman

Richard Schwartz, Iaşi, pupil

Herşcu Burăch, Iaşi, upholsterer

Isac Idelovici, Iaşi, watchmaker

Isac Cratestene, Iaşi, pupil – Mireşti–Roman

Sloim Cratestene, Iaşi, pupil – Mireşti – Roman

Solomon Butnaru, Iaşi, pupil – Mireşti – Roman

Avram Moise Grinstein, Iaşi

Bernard Zeida, Iaşi

Elias Davidsohn, Iaşi

Michel Idel, Iaşi, Mirceşti–Roman

Sulim Poker, Iaşi

[Page 172]

Haim Waisman, Iaşi

Fildman Avram Michel, Iaşi, hatter

Marcel Fichel, Darabani, tailor, Roman

Emil Schuman, Iaşi, merchant

Iţic Haim, Iaşi, carpenter –

(*The period of a great tribulation*, part I, Bucharest, 1997, p. 271–285)

Appendix No. 27 5 July – 3 Aug 1941, Forced labor, Radomir estate – Romanați.

Mr. President,

The undersigned below, Leon Segall (Leiba David), resident of the town of Roman, Panaite Donici St. No. 11, have the honor to inform you of the content of the attached memorandum, signed by the group of Jews who worked during the summer of 1941 at the estate Radomir, the propriety of Mrs. Radian, of the village Radomir, Romanați County.

In the names of the Jews below, I have the honor to ask you to intervene at Mrs. Radian, the owner of the Radomir estate, from Romanați County, to ask her to acquit our financial rights, based on the cost of living index and the wages norm for a laborer of that year.

With respect,

(signature)

To the Honorable,

Mr. President of the Romanian Jewish Union, București

Memorandum

Concerning the Jews who worked at the Radomir estate, of the village Radomir, Romanați County, the property of Mrs. Radian, in the summer of 1941.

[Page 173]

The undersigned below, Jews from the Roman County, being brought in the summer of 1941from the camp at Tg. Jiu to the Romanați County, were allocated to work at the Radomir estate, the property of Mrs. Radian in the above village, where we have worked without being paid.

We have carried out all the labors required in this season as: weeding, scything, gathering the harvest from the field, then thrashing and storing. Along these works, we also had to take care of and fatten about 150 York pigs, grown up for commerce.

The way we have carried out our work is attested by a document received from Mrs. Radian herself, the owner of the estate, whose copy is in our possession. The treatment we received at the time we have worked at this estate was of the most inhuman possible.

The administrator of the estate was assisted by the steward, a German, by the foreman Trică and by the brother of the administrator. Lately, those fervent Hitlerism sympathizers terrorized us by derision, beatings and labor beyond our capabilities – among us being persons of 55– 60 years of age.

Our labor started at 3 AM, and would end at 9, half past nine and sometimes even 10 PM. We were required to work also on Sundays. Our food consisted of 150 grams of barley bread, without any tea in the morning, and at lunch and evening pumpkin or green beans mush, with mamaliga (corn porridge).

We received meat only 2 or 3 times, of pigs dead as a result of different illnesses, that were boiled to make soap; this is the kind of meat we received,

[Page 174]

and it caused many of us to become ill. We did not receive any medical treatment, although many of us were sick. Only one person received medical assistance; he had become blind by the "porzol" powder used on the grains, and he was not able to work.

Our accommodations were in a warehouse with broken walls and floor, where the wind and rain got in without any hindrance.

Because of the lack of any ability to clean ourselves, lice roamed all over our bodies and on the straw we laid down. We haven't been paid for the labor we have performed.

(Following 37 signatures)

The Notary of the Radomir village
No.
3 Aug 1941

We attest that during the whole time from 5 July to 3 August 1941, the Jews noted in the table below have behaved well, and worked in good conditions at the estate Onor, owner Radian, in this village. The owner was questioned by us several times about their behavior at work, and she has affirmed that she was very pleased with them, and they declared that during this period they were treated well by the owner.

3 Aug 1941,
Notary (signature, undecipherable)

[Page 175]

Local council of the Radomir village,
District Câmpului,
Romanați County

List Of Jews working at Mrs. Radian's estate, and established in the village:

Froim Vigder

Moisă L. Hudea

Moisă F. Hudea

Mendel Z. Hudea

Solomon F. Hudea

Ioină Feinstein

Strul Iliescu

Iosif Kahane

Haim Iţic Nehemne

Herşcu Leiba

Leiba I. Leiba

Iosif Soifer

Iuda Faier

Isac Lupu

Moisă Soifer

Leon zis David Soifer

Benţin Gabor

Solomon Nijniver

Avram I. Fonea

Smil Leibovici

Solomon Iţicovici

Lazăr Herşcu

Iancu Iosub

David B. Pincu

David Buium

Marcu Cramer

Iosif Strul

[Page 176]

Leibovici Strul

Aron Aron

undecipherable

Pascal Avram

Pascal Zisu

Iancu Moisă

Iancu Rosenfeld

Iosif Abramovici

Smil Marcu

Leiba Moisă

Şmil Brucar

Moisă Herşcu

Smil Ghedale

Blumenfeld Haim

Katz Strul

Herşcu Lazăr

Ionă Herşcu

Iosif Leibovici

Bercovici Herman

Rosentzveig M. Itzac

Rosentzveig H. Marcu

Iţic Rotenberg

Solomon Rotenberg

Iosub Rotenberg

David Leiba a.k.a. Segall

Iosub Iosub

Iosub Simonv

Avram Goldman

We certify the present table

Mayor (undecipherable) Notary (undecipherable)

Archive F.C.E.R. Bucureşti, Center for History of the Jews in Romania, Roman File.

[Page 177]

Appendix no. 28 1942 – Jews exempted from forced labor

1. List of pharmacists and druggists from the Roman County

Beniş Raşela, Faculty of Pharmacy, age 26.

Brucmaer Zalman, Pharmacy and Biological Chemistry Faculty, age 36.

Cofler Florica, Pharmacy faculty, Iaşi, age 34.

Flexer Lipa, Pharmacy and Biological Chemistry Faculty, age 43.

Clicman Iosef, Pharmacy and Biological Chemistry Faculty, age 36.

Glicman Silvia, Pharmacy faculty, Bucureşti, age 25.

Morowitz Iosef, Pharmacy faculty, Iaşi, age 54.

Iosepovici Solomon, Pharmacy faculty, Bucureşti, age 40.

Kaufman Ioseph, Pharmacy faculty, Iaşi, age 35.

Lobel Bercu, Pharmacy faculty, Iaşi, age 37.

Marcu Iţic, Pharmacy faculty, Bucureşti, age 34.

Rosenberg Israel, Pharmacy faculty, Bucureşti, age 28.

Rămureanu Charlotte, Pharmacy faculty, Bucureşti, 31 ani

Weintraub Ozias, Ph.D. in Pharmacy - Torino, age 37.

Posmantir I. Pharmacy faculty, age 41.

2. List of Jewish physicians from the Roman County

Aroneanu Ana, born 19 Jan 1912, obstetrician

Avram Vigder, age 30, physician

Benţin Hascal, born at 10 Dec 1910, general physician

[Page 178]

Bozianu Iosub, born at 21 Sep 1899 (arrested in Transnistria) –

Cahane Leizer, born at 7 Sep 1907, physician

Cahane Rahi, born at 11 Aug 1910, physician

Dulbergher Marcel, born at 7 Jan 1908, arrested in Transnistria, physician

Dulbergher Leoni, born at 4 Jun 1911, obstetrician

Friedman Oscar, born at 24 May 1903, general physician

Faer Ana, age 31, physician

Ghertner Iancu (Iacob), born at 12 Dec 1911, general physician

Iosepovici Maer, physician, arrested in Transnistria

Ioseph Abraham, born at 6 Aug 1904, general physician

Leiba Moise, age 35, physician

Leiba Leon, age 29, physician

Leizer Bercu, age 40, physician

Moser Ghidale, age 38, physician

Ross Vasile, age 38, physician

Rosen Herman, age 30, physician

Rămureanu Aurel, age 43, physician, sent to Floreşti troop

Reznic Maier Maier, age 45, physician

Wechsler Avram, age 61, physician

Wacher Iose, age 63, physician

Welt Leivi, age 34, medic

3. List of Jewish dentists

Brand Lupu, age 51, dentist

Catz Jean, age 42, dentist

Daniel Mauriciu, age 45, dentist

Neuman David, age 52, dentist

[Page 179]

4. List of dental technicians

Avramescu Moritz, b. 1897

Daniel Ionel, b. 1919

David Mina, b. 1904

Daniel Mitică, b. 1924

Grunstein Leon, b. 1918

Herşcovici Leon, b. 1910

Herşcovici Bercu, b. 1926

Ianculovici Seina, b. 1912

Laiman Lazăr, b. 1921

Marcu Manoil, b. 1915

Nuhăm Michel a.k.a. Rintzler, b. 1915

Rosenfeld Isac, b. 1920

Rudich Meilich, b. 1921

Staerman Moritz, b. 1906

Saraga Izu, b. 1922

Zalman Selu, b. 1924

Zaltzman Maier, b. 1910

5. List of Jewish engineers

Avramescu Leon, b. 1899, chemical engineer

Beer Camille, b. 1896, chemical engineer

Hascal Herman, b. 1916, civil engineer, requisitioned by C.F.R.

Kendler Herman, age 36, engineer

Davidovici Abraham, age 41, engineer

Ivanovitz Alexandru, b. 1904, chemical engineer

6. List of lawyers

Beram Uşer, age 39

Bayer Aizic,

[Page 180]

Chisler Simon, age 30

Friedman Bernhard, age 42

Ghertner Avram, age 33

Herşcovici Saul, age 47

Herşcovici David, age 33

Maer Iosub, age 31

Marcel Iancu, age 29

Schor Maximilian, age 49

Cramer Arnold, age 45

7. List of Jewish accountants

Avram Lupu, b. 1912

David Milu, b. 1922, arrested

Gerşin Avram, b. 1904, arrested

Leibovici Elias, b. 1913, arrested

Merling Moses, b. 1899, arrested

Riva Iancu, b. 1923, arrested in Dorohoi

Strulovici Strul, b. 1914, arrested

Scharf Adela, b. 1912

Solomon Ioil, b. 1914, arrested

Braunstein Saim, b. 1909

Goldenberg Sami, b. 1904, arrested

Haimsohn Iancu, b. 1921

Locăr Sigmund, b. 1902

Maier Leon, b. 1897

Rintzler Mendel, b. 1902

Solomon Talic, b. 1902

Segal Ilie, b. 1913

Toper Noe, b. 1906, arrested

(A.S.N.F.C.E.R., file 17/1942, P. 2)

[Page 181]

Appendix no. 29, Jews from Roman evacuated to Transnistria, for insubordination to forced labor

Wachter Iosub

Wachter Ana

Herşcu Şmil

Noech Seindla

Tejghetaru Estera

Tejghetaru Moise, deceased

Tejghetaru Felicia

Tejghetaru Janeta, deceased

Tejghetaru Moise Leib, born in Transnistria

Schwartz Riven, deceased

Schwartz Rivca, deceased

Schwartz Lena, deceased

Herşcu Leiba Sapse

Herşcu Ana

Herşcu Iosub

Herşcu Eva

Herşcu Janeta

Ciortan Iancu, deceased

Leiba I. HERŞCU, deceased

Teitelbaum Mates

Teitelbaum Reghina

Teitelbaum Seiva

Teitelbaum Estera

Teitelbaum Burăch

Teitelbaum Avram

Croitoru Eliezer

CroitoruZlata

Croitoru Matilda

Croitoru Paulina

[Page 182]

Croitoru Lică

Croitoru Lucica

Croitoru Beni

Ioil Mendel

Ioil Ruchla

Mina Iancu

Noech Slima

Noech Iţic Iosub

(A.S.N.F.C.E.R., file 86/1942)

Appendix number 30, 1942, Documents pertaining to the Zionist activity in Roman

a.Greetings,

County Office of the Central Jewish (org.) in Romania – Roman

Conforming to directives no. 88 from May 28, 1942 of the Zionist Organization of Romania, Bucharest Central Bureau and no. 4981/1942 of the Central Jewish (org.), addressed to you, we have the honor to inform you that we decided to start again the activity of the local section of the Zionist Organization of Romania under the leadership of a small committee, formed from persons well known for their Zionist sentiments and who were also active in the past in this organization with enthusiasm. For this purpose, we ask you to kindly do all within you power vis–à–vis the legal authorities, so that we may obtain authorization to continue our activity, noting also that our section was previously authorized by decree of the 7th Onor Division (General Staff) no. 9782 from August 20, 1939.

[Page 183]

The committee, after filling the necessary paperwork of course, will be comprised of the following persons: Dr. M. Reznic, Leo Rohrlich, Rabbi Mendel Frenkel, Iosub Leizerovici, W. Schweitzer, Isac Rubinstein and Solomon Sabo.

At the same time with the renewal of the Zionist activity, we will reopen our organization's library, which is now being inventoried. The library is presently located in the Senior Citizens' Home. For your full information, we have the honor of attaching a copy of directive no. 88/942 of the Zionist organization of Romania and order no. 9782/939 of the 7thOnor Division (General Staff) through which the Roman organization was authorized to continue its activities.

As far as the location is concerned, once we will have the legal authorization we will establish that with the agreement of the Community president, in the Senior Citizens' Home or one of the Community offices.

With distinguished Zionist greetings, Dr. Reznic

b. (copy)

7th Division (General Staff)
No. 9782/20 August 1939
Roman

To the Zionist office Roman

With honor we bring to your attention that Mr. General Commander approved the continuation of the Roman office under the leadership presented by you in the attached list.

[Page 184]

Also, the library's activity was approved in the locale indicated by you. Authorization no. 10.456/939 will be returned shortly to the Commandment.

By order.
Chief of General Staff
Captain N. Iorga
Head of Office 2,
Captain V. Bontaş

c. Telephone 4–22–86
371–02
Bucharest, 28–May–1942
9 Anton Pan St.

Dr. M. Reznic, Roman

We have the honor to inform you that the Central Jewish (office) of Romania communicated to us through letter no. 4384 from 07 May 1942, that the Government Representative for the regulation of Jewish affairs created by order no. 1801, K. D.L. from 30 Apr 1942, saw it fit to grant the Zionist organization of Romania permission to continue its activities.

Your local county office was also informed by the Central (office) through letter no. 4981/1942.

The activity will comprise professional re–training and culture. The cultural activity will be under the Cultural Department of our Organization "Tarbut".

[Page 185]

For professional re–training (hachsharah) you will contact members of the County office of the Community, who will give you their full cooperation.

The cultural activity will comprise general Jewish culture and you shall insist in particular on Hebrew language courses for young people and adults.

We want to bring to your attention in particular that for any kind of demonstration you will need authorization from your local authorities, which you will approach through your County office.

If the authorities will not permit reunions or courses, you will have to forgo them, until such time as legal authorization will be obtained.

We also need to inform you that the activities of Keren Hayesod and Keren Kayemeth [JNF] are suspended. We wait for confirmation that you received this letter and information on the above mentioned issues.

We ask you at the same time to please send us a list of your committee's leadership.

With Zionist greetings,

President   Secretary

M. Benvenisti   I. Littman

For conformity   J. Leizerovici

(A.S.N.F.C.E.R., file 40/1942)

[Page 186]

Appendix no. 31, 1942 – 1943, Property repossessions of the Roman (Jewish) Community

a. We, Titus Dragoş, under secretary minister of State for Romanization, Colonization and Inventory;

Considering the provision of law no. 499, published in the Official Monitor no. 152 from July 3, 1942.

Considering the notice from the Government Representative for the regulation of the affairs of the Jews in Romania, communicated in no. 5312 R.D.L./942

Have decided:

Art. 1. It is declared that the building in Roman, no. 3 Miron Costin St., which belongs to the Jewish Community, is transferred to the ownership of the National Office for Romanization.

Art. 2. The Director General of the National Office for Romanization is given the task of enforcing the present decision and all the legal formalities, listed in law no. 499 / 3 July 1942.

Dated 19 Nov 1942

Subsecretary of the minister of State, Titus Dragoş

No. 87.944/M.O., P.I. no. 278 / 26 November 1942, p. 10397

b. We, undersecretary minister of State for Romanization, Colonization and Inventory.

Considering the provision no. 199 published in the Official Monitor no. 152 from July 3, 1942;

[Page 187]

Considering the favorable notice of the Government Representative for Jewish problems, communicated in directive no. 6650 R.D.L. from 1942

Have decided:

Art. 1 It is declared that the following buildings, property of the Jewish Community, situated in Roman County are transferred to the ownership of the National Office for Romanization.

1. The Community Main Office, storage, including the residence of the secretary from Principatele Unite St. no. 26
2. The Community Bathhouse, Principatele Unite St. no. 28
3. The Israelite Hospital, Principatele Unite St. no. 30
4. The Israelite Senior Citizens Home, General Manu St. no. 30
5. The residence (Senior Citizens Home building) Sucedava St. no. 3
6. The building of the Zingher donation, Aprodul Arbore S. no. 28
7. The building (Cneses Israel), Mavrichi St. no. 15
8. The building formerly The Fraternity, Regală St. no. 10–12
9. The building of the Hecht donation, General Macarovici St. no. 5
10. The building of the Weisman donation, Ştefan cel Mare St. no. 96
11. Chicken slaughterhouse, Miron Costin St. no. 5
12. Girls' elementary school, cafeteria, Sucedava St. no. 79
13. "Moske" synagugue, Vlad Ţepeş St. no. 2
14. "Croitorilor" synagogue, Vlad Ţepeş St. no. 4 (tr, note: Tailors' synagogue)
15. "Spiwak" synagogue, Vlad Ţepeş St. no. 5
16. Cismarilor" synagogue, Vlad Ţepeş St. no. 10 (tr. note: Shoemakers' synagogue)
17. "Gershin" synagogue, Sucedava St. No. 62
18. "Leizerovici" synagogue, Panaite Donici St. no. 17B
19. "Feider" synagogue, Bogdan Dragoş St. no. 58
20. "Rabbi Lewy" synagogue, Aprodul Purice St. no. 7
21. "Leipzigher" synagogue, Regala St. no. 18
22. "Branisteanu" synagogue, Aprodul Arbore St. no. 11
23. "Keilei–Iacob" synagogue, Sucedava St. no. 189

24. "Rinţler" synagogue, Logofătul Tăutu St. no. 8

25. "Kalman Leizer" synagogue, Ghica Vodă St. no. 14

26. Israelite Cemetery, Bogdan Dragoş St. no. 188

Art. 2 Mr. Director General of the National Office for Romanization is given the task of enforcing the present decision and of all the legal formalities, listed in law no. 499 / 3 July 1943.

Dated 04 Feb 1943
Subsecretary minister of State, Titus Dragoş
No. 111.248
M.O., P.I. no. 90 from 16 Apr 1943, p. 3413

c. We, Titus Dragoş, undersecretary minister of State for Romanization, Colonization and Inventory,

Considering the provisions of the law–decree no. 499/942;

Considering the notice of the Government representative for Jewish problems, communicated through no. 13.336 from R.D.L from 1943

Have decided:

Art. 1 The following buildings, property of the Jewish Community of Roman, are transferred to the ownership of the National Office for Romanization:

[Page 189]

The synagogue from Sucedava Str. No. 113

The synagogue from Sucedava Str. No. 167

Art. 2 Mr. Director General of the National Office for Romanization is given the task of enforcing the present decision and the provisions from the law–decree no. 499 from 1942.

Given on 26–Jul–1943
Subsecretary minister of State, Titus Dragoş
No. 46.094
M.O., P.I. no. 176 30–Jul–1943, p. 6727

(*Anti–Jewish Legislation*, Hasefer Publishing p. 441, 446–7, 480, Bucharest, 1993)

Appendix No. 32, 1944, *Forced Labor effectuated by Jews in Roman*

Mister Engineer.

The undersigned Jews, formerly mobilized for forced labor at the Roman National Roads Service in Batal, 55 Pioneri Sagna St. with profound respect we are asking the following:

With due respect, since you understand our tragedy and our needs, you generously agreed at the beginning of this month, as you visited our work place in Sagna, to promise us that the Roads Service will pay us for the days we worked in the month of May current.

The value of our pay is 48, 006 Lei, a negligible sum for the Service that you lead, but for each of us it means food for our families for several days. Trusting your sentiments of

[Page 190]

benevolence, we respectfully ask you to agree to pay us the above mentioned sum one hour earlier. We also ask that you empower our friend in this Detachment, Leiba David, whom we trust completely and who knows us and our places of living, to convey us the payment.

With respectful thanks, please accept our consideration,

Tobias Filip

Hudea Moise

Handelman Bercu

Hascal Hamer

Bercovici Iţic

Undecipherable

Baraf Haim

Waisman Bernard

Clikman Iancu

Corn Pincu

Cicher (Cifer?) David

Bergher Moses

Aron R. Aron

Aizik Nachman

Canamichel David

David Moise

Herşcu Aizer

Chiva Zingher

Leiba David

Pinchas M. Saea

Strul Lupu

[Page 191]

Lupu Noe

Bercu S.M. Saea

Gerşin Lazăr

Simşa Mendel

Schweitzer Bercu

Solomon Lupu

Schwartz Elly

Faibiş Casapu

David P. Pincu

Alter Lupu

Nusen David

Ghimper Herşcu

Leizer Saim

Horodniceanu Uşer

Iurgern Moses

Marcovici Simon

Rosenberg Artur

Ianci Iţic

Herşcu Iancu

Lăcătuşu Wolf

Dascălu Lazăr

Croitoru Avram

Leiba Moise

Nehemia Iancu

Moscovici Nathan

Solomon Herman

Ghertner Hascal

Lazarovici Isidor

Vital A. Iţic

Rachmil Iţic

Undecipherable

Ghertner Avram

[Page 192]

Chetreanu Leiba

Braunstein Samoil

Faider Bercu

Iosub Iancu

Avram Rubin

Avram Fonea

Barbălat Benzin

Herşcovici Herman

Iohan Iosef

Leibovici David

Leibovici Froim

Leibovici Max

Meilich Marcu

Strul David

Haim Strul

Herşcovici Smil

Locăr Izrail

Miremberg Marcu

Sufaru Avram

Lazăr Marcus

Landsbergher Moise

Leiba Iancu

Iţic Ihiel

Leib S. Iţic

Cramer S. Veller

Rintzler Nelu

Faibiş Buium

Ghidali Iosub

Faibiş Iancu

Sufăr Samoil

Vainştein Beer

Săpcaru Bercu

[Page 193]

Taler Strul

Nusen Moise

20 August 1944

To the Respected

Engineer Chief of the Roman National Roads Service

(A.R.F.C.E.R., Bucharest, Center Of theHistory of the Jews in Romania, Roman File)

Appendix No. 33, 1977, *Confirmation of Jewish merchants, craftsmen and industrialists in Roman*

1.	Grain merchants	10
2.	Flour merchants	3
3.	Food merchants	8
4.	Cattle merchants	2
5.	Iron merchants	12
6.	Watches and jewellery merchants	8
7.	Shoes and accessories merchants	12
8.	Radio and electric appliances merchants	5
9.	Glass and China merchants	8
10.	Paints merchants	4
11.	Stationary and paper merchants (Beram Ozias and Brizel Solomon)	2
12.	Printing merchants (Grunberg Leon Grunberg Isidor Abramovici M. Herş Simensohn Michel Rivensohn Calman Beram Zalman Baratz Israel)	7
13.	Wood and construction material merchants	7

[Page 194]

14.	Agents, commission, insurance, lottery	4
15.	Wood merchants	8
16.	Textile & haberdashery merchants	39
17.	Clothing merchants	8

Craftsmen: furriers – 4; shoemakers – 32; saddlers – 8; harness–makers – 5; coopers – 7; ironsmiths – 4; electricians, radio–technicians, drivers, plumbers – 18; locksmiths – 15; bookbinders – 3; carpenters – 22; tailors – 36; printers – 12; tinsmiths – 11; painters – 2; house–painters – 2; chemical laundry – 2; upholsterers – 5; photographers – 4 (Avramescu Aurel, Avramescu Iosif, Barmac Iţic, Schwartz Suchăr); bakers – 13.

Manufacturers:

Tin and wire: Seider Iosef, Dr. Rosen Herman, Leibovici Iancu, Kendler Herman

Military equipment: Stumer Iancu

Soap: Bernthal Iosef, Margulies Avram, Margulies Moriţ

Ropes: Grimberg Samoil

Oil factory: Grimberg Samoil, Grimberg Moriţ, Grimberg Iţic

Lumber works, sawmills: Straucher Moritz, Straucher Vili, Straucher Iosif

(A.S.N.F.C.E.R, File No. 31 / 1947)

[Page 195]

Notes

A. The Demographic Development of the Jews of Roman and Surroundings

1. Ion Bojoi–Ioniță Ichim – *Județul Neamț,* [*The Neamtz County,*] Academy Press, R. S. R., București 1974, p. 97

2. Bishop Melchisedec–Útefanescu – *Cronica Romanului și a Episcopiei de Roman,* [*The Chronicle of Roman and the Roman Diocese*] vol. I, București, 1874 p. 37; Pompei Gh. Samaran – *Medicina și farmacia în trecutul românesc 1382–1775,* [*Medicine and Pharnacy in the Romanian past* 1382–1775]vol. I, Călărași, p. 245

3. Domnița Hordila – Populația Romanului în primele sale veacuri de existență [The population of Roman in the first centuries of its existence] in: *Istoria orașului Roman,* [*The History of the City of Roman*] Roman, 1992, p. 58

4. *Izvoare și mărturii privind evreii din România* ("I.M.E.R.") [*Sources and Testimonies regarding the Jews of Romania*] II/1, București, 1998, p. 217

5. "I.M.E.R." I, București, 1986, p. 111

6. Melchisedec cited work, p. 37; "I.M.E.R." II/I, p. 16

7. Domnița Hordila, cited article

8. "I.M.E.R." II/1, p. 158

9. Ibidem, p. 170

10. Ibidem, p. 17, 160

11. Idem, II/2, p. 58

12. S. Svemer – *Falstendige chronologie fin der idișe gheșichte* (Yiddish), Iași, part I, 1923, p. 103; Paul Cernodoveanu "Evreii în epoca fanariotă" ["The Jews in the Phanariot Era"] "Magazin istoric" ["History Magazine"], March, 1997

13. M. Schwartzfeld – Vechimea evreilor în Moldova și Valahia ["The antiquity of the Jews in Moldova and Valachia"] in "Analele Societății Iuliu Barasch" ["The Annals of the Iulius Barasch Society"], III/1889, p. 117

14. P. G. Dimitrev – *Moldova în epoca feudalismului. Recensămintele Moldovei în anii 1772, 1773 și 1774*, [*Moldova in the Feudal era. Moldova Censes in 1772, 1773, and 1774*] vol VII, part II, Chişinău, 1975

15. P. Racanu "Lefile boierilor Moldovei în 1776" ["The Salaries of the Moldovan Boyars in 1776"], Iaşi, 1887

16. Dan Ripa–Buicliu – N. Capsali–Vasilescu "Un document cămătăresc" ["An usurious document"] in "An. Inst. Ist. Iaşi" ["Annals of the Jassy Historical Institute"], 1997 ; "I.M.E.R" II/2, p. 349

17. Melchisedec cited work, part II, Bucureşti, 1875, p. 155, 156

18. Axelrad "Popa şi ovreiul" ["The Priest and the Jew"] "Curierul israelit" ["Israelite Courier"]/5.X.1937; Dr. V. Gomoi – Repertor de medici, farmacişti, veterinari din ţinuturile româneşti înainte de 1870 [Index of physicians, pharmacists and veterinarians in the Romanian Counties before 1870], vol. I, indicates the exact year

19. Epifanie Cozarascu – Asistenţa medico–sanitară. Începuturile [Medical and Sanitary Assistance. The Beginnings] in: *Istoria oraşului Roman* [*The History of the City of Roman*], Roman, 1992, p. 182–183

20. M. Schwartzfeld, cited work, p. 132

21. I.M.E.R. II/2, 1991, p. 435–6

22. Ibidem, p. 445–447

23. Ibidem, p. 452–453

24. N. Iorga – *Istoria poporului românesc* [*The History of the Romanian People*], vol. II, Bucureşti, 1927, p. 213

25. N. Iorga – *Documente privitoare la familia Callimachi* [*Documents regarding the Callimachi family*], vol. I, Bucureşti, 1902, p. 536; *Bibliografia analitică a periodicelor româneşti* [*The Analitic Biography of the Romanian Periodicals*], vol. II, Bucureşti, 1970, p. 168

26. Scarlat Callimachi – S. Cris. Cristian – *Călători şi scriitori despre evreii din Principatele Româneşti* [*Travellers and Writers on the Jews in the Romanian Principalities*], Iaşi, 1935, p. 104–105 (cites Dr. Joh. Ferdinand Neigebauer – *Beschrebung der Moldau und Walachei* [*Account of Moldavia and Valachia* (German)]– Leipzig, 1848), p. 362

27. *Dezvoltarea economiei Moldovei* [*The Development of the Moldavian Economy*], 1848–1864, Bucureşti, 1963, p. 362

28. N. SUŢU – Notaţii statistice [Statistical Notes] – *Opere economice* [*Economical Works*], Bucureşti, 1957, p. 146–7

29. Analele parlamentare ale României [Anals of Romanian Parliament], Vol. XII, part II, Bucureşti, 1902, p. 533

30. Dr. Elias Schwartzfeld – From the history of the Jews – *Inpopulare-repopulare şi întemeierea târgurilor şi târguşoarelor din Moldova* [*Population–repopulation and the Establishment of the Towns and Townlets of Moldova*], Bucureşti, 1914, p. 66; I. Kara în "R.C.M.", 454/1980

31. Alex. Lahovary – *Marele dicţionar geografic al României* [*The Great Geographic Dictionary of Romania*], Bucureşti, 1898, vol. I–IV

32. Iacov bar Aşer Psantir – *Divrei haiamim leanţot Rumenie* [*The History of the Romanian Countries* (Hebrew)], Iaşi, 1871, vol. II, p. 26

33. I.S. Valentineanu *"Ebrei în România"* ["*Jews in Romania*"], Bucureşti, 1886

34. "Romanu", Roman/27.VII.1886, 6.X.1886

35. "Revista israelită" ["Israelite Review"], year I n. 18, p. 563

36. "Romanu", Roman/22.I.1888

37. Idem, 4.IX.188

38. "Revista israelită" ["Israelite Review"], year I n. 18, p. 563

39. "Anuarul naţional al României 1891–1892" ["National Year Book of Romania 1891–1892"], Bucureşti, 1892, p. 632

40. M. O. 7/11.IV.1895

41. *Documente privind istoria economică a României. Oraşe şi târguri. Moldova* [*Documents regarding the History of the Romanian Economy. Cities and Towns. Moldova*], series A, vol. II, Bucureşti, 1960; Secretariatul de Stat al Moldovei 1832–1862 [The State Secretariat of Moldova 1832–1862] (inventory)

42. Dr. G.Z. Petrescu – "Medicina publică în Moldova acum 100 de ani" ["Public Medicine in Moldova 100 years ago" in "Revista ştiinţelor medicale" ["Medical Sciences Review"], 1/1931

43. Arh. F.C.E.R., Mape Kaufman I; "Analele parlamentare ale României" [Annals of the Romanian Parliament], vol. XII, part II, Bucureşti, 1902, p.472

44. Theodor Codrescu "Uricariul" ["The Bailiff"]II, Iaşi, 1892; Marius Mircu *Croitorul din Back* [*The Tailor from Back*], Edit. Cartea Românească, Buc., 1979, p. 60

45. "Romanu", Roman/28.VIII.1883, 19.X:1883, 39.X.1883, 20.VIII.1884

46. Idem, 15.VIII.1884

47. Acad. N. Cajal – Dr. Harz Kuller (coordinators) – Dr. Liviu Rotman – *Evreii şi începuturile industriei româneşti.* [*The Jews and the Beginnings of the Romanian Industry*] ("Contribuţia evreiilor din România la cultură şi civilizaţie" ["The Contribution of the Jews of Romania to Culture and Civilization"], Bucureşti, 1996).

48. "Romanu", Roman/10.VI.1883

49. N. Iorga – *Istoria românilor prin calatori* [*The History of Romania (as related) by Travellers*], Vol. II, Bucureşti, 1925, p. 264

50. Ferdinand Johann Neugebauer – "Mănăstirile Moldovei din Carpaţi" ["Moldova's Carpathians Monasteries"] "Propăşire" ["Prosperity"], year I, n. 5/1844

51. "Romanu", Roman/24.I.1885

52. I.B. Brociner – *Chestiunea evreilor pamânteni* [*The Question of Native Jews*], Iaşi, 1901, p. 64–65

53. Leonida Colescu – Recensământul general al populaţiei României [The General Census of the Population in Romania], Bucureşti, 1905, p. XLV, XLVII, 74, 79

54. Statutele Comunităţii Israelite din Roman [The Statutes of the Israelite Community of Roman], Roman, 1905

55. Emil D.B. Vasiliu – *Situaţia demografică a României* [*The Demographic Situation of Romania*], Edit. Cartea Românească [Publishing], Cluj, 1912

56. *Problema evreiască în stenogramele Consiliului de Miniştri* [*The Jewish Problem in the Council of Ministers Reports*], Buc. 1996, p. 72, 81, 93, 99

57. Dezvoltarea economică a Moldovei... [The Economic Development of Moldova...] p. 46

58. Radu Rosetti – *Pentru ce s–au răsculat ţăranii* [*What did the Peasants Revolt for*], Edit. Eminescu, Bucureşti, 1987, p. 324

59. Gh. Matei *Răsunetul internațional al răscoalei țăranilor din 1907* [*The International Echo of the 1907 Peasants Revolt*], București, 1957, p. 170, 172, 173

60. "Diplomați italieni despre 1907" ["Italian Diplomats on 1907"] in "Magazin istoric" ["History Magazine"]/Oct. 1997

61. "Egalitatea" ["The Equality"]/6.III.1907, 30.III.1907

62. "Cronica israelită" ["The Israelite Chronicle"], VII, n. 10/10.III.1907

63. *Marea răscoală a țăranilor din 1907* [*The Great Peasants' Revolt of 1907*], Editura Academiei [Academy Press], 1987, p. 74

64. Octav Gavrilescu "1907 pe teritoriul fostului judeţ Roman" ["1907 within the Territory of the former Roman County"] in *Istoria orașului Roman* [*The History of the City of Roman*], Roman, 1992, p. 240

65. M. Schweug – *Eroismul ostășesc al evreilor în actualul război mondial* [*The Military Heroism of the Jews in the Current World War*], București, 1915

66. Dr. W. Filderman – *Adevărul asupra problemei evreiești din România în lumina textelor religioase și statisticei* [*The Truth about the Jewish Problem in Romania in the Light of the Religious Texts and the Statistics*], București, 1925, p. LXXXII. Jews of Roman that also died in the war: Solomon G.I., in the battle of Dealul Porcului, born in Gădinţi – Roman ("Revista cultului mozaic" ["The Mosaic Cult Review"], 675/15.IX.1988) = R.C.M.; Poplingher Haim, Iţic a.k.a. Isac Zilberman in the battle of Călugăreni, Leizer Strul (Strule) corporal, 4th Sanitary Company; wounded were Iancu Leiba (54th Infantry Regiment) and Mendel Smil David (Reg. 14 inf.), while Idel Moisa of the 54th Infantry Regiment was decorated with the "Crucea comemorativă" ["Commemorative Cross"] with the Mărășești strap (State Archives Neamtz, Roman Jewish Community Collection, dos. 46/1946, 64/1944)

67. "Curierul israelit" ["The Israelite Courier"]/18.VII.1934

68. "Egalitatea"["The Equality"]/12.II.1926

69. Idem, of 29.XII.1906;– I. Brand – Roman (wines), A. Schorr, N. Sanilovici – Roman (spirits) also won bronze medals with honors ("Egalitatea" ["The Equality"]/19.I.1907)

70. M.O. 213/12.IX.1936 și M.O. 243/19.X.1936

71. "Gazeta evreiască" ["The Jewish Gazette"]/18.VI.1943 and "Curierul israelit" ["The Israelite Courier"]/13.III.1932

72. *Istoria oraşului Roman* [*The History of the City of Roman*], Roman, p. 266,268

73. Arhivele Statului fil. Neamţ, Com. Evr. Roman [The State Archives, Neamtz branch, Jewish Community Roman] Register 1/1020, dos. 103/1945, dos. 31/1947

74. Idem, dos. 9/1940, dos. 47/1942–1943

75. Matatias Carp/*Cartea neagră – Fapte şi documente – Suferinţele evreilor din România – 1940–1944* [*The Black Book – Facts and Documents – The Suffering of the Jews in Romania – 1940–1944*], Bucureşti 1946, vol. I, p. 156

76. Arh. Stat. Neamţ, Com. Evr. Roman, [The State Archives, Neamtz branch, Jewish Community Roman] dos. 30/1941

77. S.C. Cristian – *Patru ani de urgie* [*Four Years of Wrath*], Bucureşti, no year, p. 127

78. Arh. Stat. Neamţ, Com. Evr. Roman, [The State Archives, Neamtz branch, Jewish Community Roman] dos. 25, 27, 28, 29/1941

79. Idem, dos. 64/1943

80. Idem, dos. 38/1943

81. Idem, dos. 37/1943

82. Idem, dos. 40/1942–1943

83. Idem, dos. 49/1943

84. Idem, dos. 38/1943

85. Idem, dos. 68/1943

86. S.C. Cristian, cited work, p. 81

87. Arh. Stat Neamţ, Comunitatea Evreilor Roman, [The State Archives, Neamtz branch, Jewish Community Roman] dos. 79/1944

88. Idem, dos. 80/1944

89. Idem, dos. 81/1944

90. Idem, dos. 82/1944

91. S. Cris. Cristian, cited work, p. 80

92. *Perioda unei mari restrişti* [*The Period of a Great Tribulation*], Bucureşti, 1997, Hasefer Publishing, part I, p. 453

93. Legislația antievreiască [The Anti–Jewish Legislation] , București, 1993, Hasefer Publishing, p. 441, 446, 475, 480

94. *Perioda unei mari restriști* [*The Period of a Great Tribulation*] , part II, p. 115

95. Ibidem, p. 290

96. Matatias Carp, cited work, vol III, p. 42

97. Arh. Stat. Neamț Comunitatea evr., Roman [The State Archives, Neamtz branch, Jewish Community Roman], dos. 92/1944

98. Ibidem

99. Idem, dos. 86/1944

100.   Arh. Stat. Neamț, Serv. Sanitar Roman [The State Archives, Neamtz branch, Sanitary Service Roman], dos. 4/1942, p. 46

101.   Idem, Com. Evr. Roman [Jewish Community Roman], dos. 92/1944

102.   Idem, dos. 64/1944

103.   *Legislația antievreiască* [*The Anti–Jewish Legislation*] – photo

104.   Arh. Stat. Neamț, Com. Evr. Roman [The State Archives, Neamtz branch, Jewish Community Roman], dos.99/1944

105.   Idem

106.   Arh. Stat. Neamț, Serviciul sanitar Roman [The State Archives, Neamtz branch, Sanitary Service Roman], dos.2 4/1941

[Page 201]

Notes (cont.)

B. The Jewish Community of Roman throughout time

1. Suchard Rivenzon, The Jewish School of the Village of Roman, Printer Beram, Father, Roman, 1943, p. 5.

2. Sami Wechsler– Contributions to the Monograph of the Jewish Community of Roman 1928, ms.).

3. "Îfrăţirea" (Brotherhood), year II, no. 43/ August 8, 1887.

4. "Revista Israelită" (Jewish Magazine), year V, no. 11/ June 15, 1890.

5. "Egalitatea" (Equality), XVIII, no. 4/26 January, 1907.

6. "Curierul israelit" (The Jewish Courier), year II no. 63 /April 19, 1908.

7. "Neamul evreiesc" (The Jewish Nation), no. 8 / May 15, 1910.

8. "Dimineaţa" (The Morning), year XXII, no. 5094 / September 23, 1920.

9. "Renaşterea noastră" (Our Rebirth), no. III, no. 162 / March 5, 1927.

10. The almanac of the newspaper "Tribuna evreiască" (The Jewish Tribune) for the year 5698 (1937), Iaşi, 1937. In 1936, the Jewish Community Committee was composed of: President – Attorney Arnold Cramer, Secretary – M. Rintzler and Members – Attorney A. Ghertner, David Laufer, M. Schaechter, Zalman Bercovici, Iancu Poilici, Avraham Hecht, Michel Brucmaier, Solomon Beram, I. Bentin, Smaie Aizic, Haim Smilovici, Avram Solomon, Lazăr Barasch and Moty Pinsler.

11. "Renaşterea noastră" (Our Rebirth), year XVI, no. 711/ May 18, 1940.

12. State Archives, Neamţ, Funds of the Jewish Community of Roman. (A.S.N.F.C.E.R.), file 24/1941; President of the Roman County C. E. R. was Mauriciu Daniel and Secretary General was Mauriciu Rosenberg.

13. "Curierul Israelit" (The Israelite Courier) / June 19, 1932, "Annals of the Jews of Romania", 1937.

14. Sami Wecsler, op. cit.

15. Mendel Frenkel, op. cit. (Monograph of the Jewish Community of Roman ms.).

16. "Neamul evreiesc" (The Jewish Nation) no. 9/ May 22, 1910.

17. A.S.N.F.C.E.R., file 10/1941.

18. Anti Jewish Legislation...p. 446; "Şoarei" synagogues are mentioned as well.

19. A.S.N.F.C.E.R., file 44/1942, Tefila Ţedek, Poalei Ţedek and 2 Beit-Tefila

20. Iţic Kara "Rabbis and scholars in Moldavian communities" in "R.C.M.", 269/I.II.1972; "Israelite Magazine", year II, no. 7, p. 194–197; Jewish Cemetery of Piatra Neamţ (Pincu Pascal), "Jewish Reality" no. 11/1995, Archives of the Jewish Community Piatra Neamţ, State wages C.E.R./42.

21. Sami Wecsler, op. cit.

22. "Revista Israelită" (Israelite Magazine), na. II, no. 7/1887 p. 196.

23. Ibidem

24. Idem no. 3, p. 79; Bogdan Dragoş Street Cemetery inaugurated in 1849. In its center there exists an imposing monument in memory of heroes, inaugurated in 1925 in the presence of local authorities, and the chapel consists of a ceremonial room and a room for the cleansing of the remains. There was also an area to store the coffins (Mendel Frenkel, op. cit.).

25. Eliezer The Pinkas [Register] of the Jewish Community of Roman"/"R.C.M." no. 103 of April 1964.

26. "Social Historic Annals – Iuliu Barasch" / March 1889, p.79.

27. "Revista Israelită" (Israelite Magazine), year II, no. 8, p. 221, "Egalitatea" (Equality), year II, no. 21/ May 29, 1892.

28. Mendel Frankel, op.cit.

29. Neamţ, State Archives, Neamţ County Health Services, file 10/1904.

30. "Egalitatea" (Equality) no. 34/ August 31, 1901.

31. "Propăşirea [Prosperity], scientific and literary journal", year I, Sunday August 13, 1844.

32. Ministry of Public education and Culture – School Houses –"The Golden Book of Donors 1851–1901", Bucharest, 1901, p. 276, 223.

33. M.O. no. 19 / December 31, 1879.

34. "Roman", Roman / June 18, 1887, "Egalitatea" (Equality) September 1, 1906.

35. "Revista Israelită" (Israelite Magazine), year II, no. 13.

36. "Egalitatea" (Equality) / December 22, 1900.

37. Idem December 15, 1900.

38. Dr. Iacob Felix, "Istoria igienei in Romania" (The history of hygiene in Romania) in the "Annals of the Romanian Academy", 2nd series, Tome XXIV, The scientific section Memoirs, 2nd Part, 2nd Memoir, Bucharest, 1902, p. 34.

39. Mendel Frankel, op. cit.; Sami Wecsler, op. cit.

40. Dr. Epifanie Cozărăscu, "The beginnings of health aid in Roman" (Roman Israelite Hospital), in *New and Old Hospitals*, Medical Edition (editor Dr. G. Brătescu) Bucharest, 1976, p. 103–104.

41. Sami Wecsler, op. cit.

42. Dr. Epifanie Cozărăscu, op. cit.

43. Sami Wecsler, op. cit., "Egalitatea" (Equality) / January 11, 1902.

44. "Fraternitatea" (The Fraternity) / July 5, 1885.

45. Dr. Epifanie Cozărăscu, op. cit., p. 105, Victor Gomoiu, op. cit., vol. I, p. 357.

46. Paul Pruteanu, Contributions to the History of Moldavian Hospitals, Bucharest, 1957, p. 19.

47. Dr. Epifanie Cozărăscu, op. cit., p. 106, "Revista Israelită" (Israelite Magazine), year II, no. 7, p. 194–197.

48. State Archives, Iaşi, Funds of the Health Committee, Transport 1757, opis 2005, file 209/1859.

49. "Romanu" [The Roman], Roman / January 24, 1885.

50. Dr. Victor Gomiu, Farm. Gh. and Marian Gomoiu – Addendum to "Listing of doctors, pharmacists and veterinarians in the Romanian counties before 1870", Bucharest, 1941 (letter L).

51. Dr. Iacob Felix – General Report regarding public hygiene and health services of the Romanian Monarchy [*Regat*] for the year 1892, Bucharest, 1893, p. 166, 172. In 1891, in Roman county was founded a hospital for sufferers of granulous conjunctivitis (trachoma), an illness often striking Jews; "Egalitatea" (Equality) / no. 15 April 18, 1908, p. 180.

52. "Gazeta Balului" (The Ball Gazette), occasional issue of the Roman Jewish Community / November 25, 1933.

53. Dr. Epifanie Cozărăscu – Medical and hygiene aid in modern times until 1945; in the *History of the City of Roman*, Roman, 1992, p. 363.

54. A.S.N.F.C.E.R., file 32/1944.

55. *A period of great restrictions*, 2nd part, p. 420.

56. Dr. Epifanie Cozărăscu, article cited in *"History of the..."* p. 364.

57. Mariana Sefer – Ethnic Elements from the XIXth century, in the archive of manuscripts of Professor Grigore Crețu, in "Microbiology, Parasitology, and Epidemiology", no. 1 January–February, no. 2 March–April, no. 3 July–August, 1971.

58. *Învățământul medical si farmaceutic din București* (Medical and Pharmaceutical Study in Bucharest), Bucharest, 1963, p.

59. State Archives, Iași, Health Committee, tr. 1434, op. 1634, file 522/1838/371; tr. 1567, file 262/1852 and inventory, "Health Committee" (1832).

60. State Archives, Iași, Committee of Health, tr. 1434, file 529/1844, 532/1846, 259/1850, tr. 1567.

61. Heinz Rohrlich "Rumänischen studenten an der Ludwig–Maximilians Universität–MÅ±nchen, in der 19 Jahrhundert" (Romanian Students at the Ludwig Maximilian University–Munich in the XIX–th Century) in "Al XII–lea Congres internațional de istoria medicinei" (The XII–th International Congress on the History of Medicine) p. 460; Neamț State Archives, Vital Statistics Roman, births 1879.

62. Neamț, State Archives, Budget of the Roman Hospital, file 4/1879.

63. Dr. P. Cazacu – I.C. Frună, Documentary material to resolve the pharmacy question in Romania, Bucharest, 1916, p. 177.

64. Heinz Rohrlich – Dr. G. Brătescu in "Revista medicală" (Medical Magazine), Tg. Mureș, no. 3/972 (in other documents he is listed as Joseph Roitman).

65. Dr. Epifanie Cozărăscu – The Roman Hospital in the First World War, in "Trecut și viitor în medicină" (Past and future in medicine), Bucharest, 1981 (edited by Dr. G. Brătescu, p. 481, 485).

66. Dr. Pharmacist Vasile I. Lipan – Istoria farmaciei in date (Chronological History of Pharmacies), Braunschwieg, 1991. From other sources we learn that in 1948 the pharmacist Iosepovici Șloim was the president of

the interim committee of the Pharmaceutical Collegiate of Roman County.

67. Sami Wecsler m.s. cit.: in 1836 there were 10 Jewish teachers in Roman (Jewish Contribution to culture, p.496); In 1880 the Community secured the operation of a school with three teachers of Hebrew and one of Romanian ("Fraternitatea" [The Fraternity] Year II, no. 30 / 1880).

68. Suchard Rivenzon, op. cit., p. 16–17, Lăcărămioara Iordachescu, Education in the History of Roman, 1992, p.302.

69. "Egalitatea" (Equality), no. 48 / 10 December, 1893.

70. Suchard Rivenzon, op. cit., p. 17, 20, 22, 26.

71. "Egalitatea" (Equality), / 24 August, 1901.

72. Idem, no. 30 / 30 July, 1904, no. 15 /18 April, 1908.

73. Idem, year XVI, no. 28 / 22 July, 1904, 10 February 1906, year XVIII, no. 2/12 January, 1907, no. 1 / 19 December, 1908; S. Rivemzon, op. cit., p. 55.

74. "Curierul Israelit" (The Israelite Courier) no. 39/10 July, 1909.

75. Suchard Rivemzon, op. cit., p. 30, 32, "Neamul evreiesc" (The Jewish Nation) year II, no. 8 / 15 May, 1910, A.S.N.F.C.E.R., file 3/1909–1910.

76. Suchard Rivenzon, op. cit., p. 37, Neamţ, State Archives, Neamţ County Health Services, file 15/1920.

77. "Curierul Israelit" (The Israelite Courier) year XVIII, no. 2 / 11 January, 1925

78. Idem, year XX no. 36 / 30 October 1927.

79. S. Rivenzon, op. cit., p. 38–41, 44, 46.

C. Welfare and mutual aid societies

1. Horia Nestorescu – Bălceşti – The Romanian Masonic Order, Bucharest, 1993, p. 9, 13, 16, 18.

2. A.D. Ştern – From the life of a Romanian Jew, vol. 1, Bucharest 1915, p. 154.

3. "Egalitatea" (Equality), / year XV, no. 8 / 20 February, 1903, in 1990 the honorary president of the "Progresul" Order was Dr. Henc.

4. "Romanu" (The Roman), Roman, 16 February, 1886, "Revista Israelită" (Israelite Magazine), year II, / 15 February, 1887.

5. "Egalitatea" (Equality), / 16 February, 1901.

6. "Curierul Israelit" (The Israelite Courier) year XIII, no. 18/ 2nd January, 1921; in 1934, the association "Iubirea de oameni" ("Love of Mankind") is mentioned, led by Noel Bring (idem 24 June, 1934).

7. "Renaşterea noastră" (Our Rebirth), year III, no. 158/5 February, 1927, A.S.N.F.C.E.R., file 91/44.

8. "Egalitatea" (Equality), / 18 January, 1902, 28 May, 1914, "Renaşterea noastră" (Our Rebirth), /14 May, 1927.

9. "Egalitatea" (Equality), / 28 February, 1903, "Curierul Zionului" (The Zion Courier) 17 February 1904.

10. A.S.N.F.C.E.R., file 91/1944.

11. "Stindardul"(The Flag) year I no. 3 / 1 September, 1882.

12. "Egalitatea" (Equality), / year XXXVII, no 25 / 18 June, 1926, "News from the Jewish World" of 20 September, 1928 (in this year the kindergarten opened, founded and maintained by A.C.F.E.), idem year VI, no. 396/2 October, 1930, "Jewish Woman" no. 45 / 5 January 1931.

13. "Mântuirea" (Redemption), year III, no. 800 / 1 September, 1921, "Renaşterea noastră" (Our Rebirth), year III, no. 169 / 30 April, 1927, "Lumea" (The World) year X, no. 2697 / 4 August, 1927, "Dimineaţa" (The Morning), / 16 June, 1928, "Curierul Israelit" (The Israelite Courier) / 28 may, 1933.

14. "The Maccabi" no. 20 / 1 September, 1934, Cernăuţi.

15. "The Maccabi Bulletin", year III, no. 17–18 / 8 February, 1935.

16. "Lumea" (The World) year X no. 2697/4 August, 1927.

17. "Egalitatea" (Equality), no. 30/2 August, 1891.

18. Idem, no. 38/3 October, 1903, "Curierul Israelit" (The Israelite Courier) /1 March, 1913.

19. "Curierul Israelit" (The Israelite Courier) year XII, no. 24 (546) / 5 March, 1920.

20. Idem, no. 16 / 8 May, 1932, 12 May, 1932.

D. The Zionist movement

1. Dr. Hary Kuller, *Eight studies on the history of the Jews of Romania*, Bucureşti, 1997, p. 231–232; on the expulsion of the Jews from the villages see "Romanu", Roman / 16 / 1883: on the law of the ambulant commerce ("Yearbook for Israelites", year VIII / 1888)

2. "Equality", year IV, no. 226 / 20 July 1893.

3. "Voice of Zion" / 16 Apr 1899

4. "Equality" / 31 Dec 1899

5. Ldem / 16 Nov 1901 (from the *shekelists*, Soc. "Cremieux")

6. Idem / 3 Jan 1903

7. Idem / 18 Apr 1903, 18 Jul 1903

8. "Ha'ivri" (the Hebrew), Brody, 7 May 1886

9. "Equality" / 12 May 1900, 2 Jun 1900, 16 Jun 1900, 30 Jun 1900

10. Dr. Th. Loewenstein – Herzl, p. 43

11. "Equality" no. 37 / 19 Sep 1903

12. "The salvation", year II no. 554 / 5 Nov 1920

13. A.S.N.F.C.E.R, file 17 / 1942

14. "Equality", year XV / 26 Nov 1904

15. Idem / 22 May 1909, 27 Nov 1909; Hary Kuller, cited book, p. 247

16. "The Israelite Courier", year XII no. 24 / 5 Mar 1920

17. "Rebirth", year I, no. 18 / 18 Jan 1925

18. "News from the Jewish life" / 19 Mar 1929

19. A.S.N.F.C.E.R., file 103 / 1945, file 40/1 942

20. "Equality" 17 Sep 1899

21. Idem, year XIII, no. 31 / 9 Aug1902, no. 50 / 27 Dec 1902, no. 6 / 7 Feb. 1903, no. 9 / 28 Feb. 1903, no. 14 / 11 Apr 1903, no. 28 / 18 Aug 1903, no. 2 / 15 Aug 1903, no. 26 / 2 Jul 1904

22. "The Zionist" I, no. 5 / 28 Jul 1906, no. 14 / 6 Jan 1907; "The Equality" / 2 May 1908, no. 47 / 4 Dec 1909

23. "The Jewish people", year XIV, no. 23–24 / 16 Oct 1921

24. The Voice of Zion" / 16 Apr 1899, 30 Apr 1899, 21 May 1899, 3 Jun 1899, "Equality" / 17 Sep 1899, "The Sunshine" / 24 Nov 1899,

Equality" / 5 Nov 1899, 25 Jul 1903, "The Israelite Chronicle", year III, no. 37 / 27 Sep 1903

25. "Equality" / 8 Oct 1899, "The Sunshine" / 8 Oct 1899, "The Courier of Zion" no. 8 / 29 Feb 1904, "Equality" / 15 Oct 1899, "The Courier of Zion", year I, no. 7 / 17 Feb. 1904, no. 11 / 21 Mar 1904

26. "The Israelite Courier" no. 38 / Sept. 1909

27. "Equality", year XXVI, no. 39 / 9 Oct 1915, "The Israelite Courier", year XII, no. 2 / 12 Sep. 1920, no. 18 / 2 Jan 1921, "The Jewish people", year XIV, no. 23–24 / 16 Oct 1921

28. "Our rebirth," year IV no. 189 / 22 Oct 1927, "Equality" / 9 Mar 1928

29. "News from the Jewish World" / 15.Jan. 1928, "Our Rebirth" / 17 Mar 1928, "R.C.M." no. 76 / Oct 1993

30. "Sami Wecsler, cited manuscript," "Hasmonaea," year XXI no. 11–12 / May–June 1940

31. "Equality" 28 Feb 1903, 2 May 1908, "News from the Jewish world" / 9 May 1940

E. Aspects of the spiritual life of the Jews of Roman and surroundings

1. "R.C.M." / 15 Sep 1987

2. Lya Benjamin, Irina Cajal–Marin, Hary Kuller – *Myths, rites and ritual objects*, București, 1994,

3. p. 90–91; Rabbi Mendel Frenkel offers additional details concerning the dress of the Jews of Roman: the *Kapote*, a long black coat, made of cloth, for Saturdays one made of silk, and on their heads, on holidays, a *shtreimel*. On the same occasions, the women wore on their heads a *sterntikhel* [lit. forehead–scarf], a kind of headband made of beads.

4. Iulian Șvarț, in " *Bucareșter șriftn*" [Bucharest Writings], vol. IV. București, 1981, p. 153; of the children games, Lazăr Șăineanu mentions: the game with the flag on *Simkhat Tora*, when on top of the flag was placed an apple with a candle, the spinning toy (dreidl), on Hanukah, the rattler (grager), on Purim (Lazăr Șăineanu, in "The annals of the Historic Society Dr. Iuliu Barasch", year III, 1889)

5. Haralamb Zincă , "Miriam" in "R.C.M." 698 / 1 Nov 1990

6. H.B. Oprisan – *The Romanian Popular theatre* Bucureşti, 1987, p. 167–169

7. Andrei Oişteanu – Mithos/Logos – *Studies and essays of cultural anthropology*, Nemira publishing house, 1998, p. 177, 178

    I.   Kara–Şvarţ, in *"Bucareşter şriftn"* [Bucharest Writings], vol. IV, Bucureşti, 1981, p. 110

8. Moişe Lax – *Literarişe notn* (Yidish) [Literary Notes], Bucureşti, p. 143, "R.C.M." / 1 Mar 1982, Israel Bercovici in " *Bucareşter şriftn*" [Bucharest Writings], I. Bucureşti, p. 98 (1978)

9. "Shevet Romania (Romanian tribe)" / 1 May 1977; collaborators at "Jerusalem" were B. Bercoff, A.H. Solomon, A. Rindman, B. Moscu, Dr. Abr. Stern: "Romanu", Roman / 29 Jan 1887, 7 May 1887, 14 Feb 1888, 1 Oct 1888

10. (Iancu Gross has also translated "The Harem woman" and "America's billionaires," Hary Kuller, *Bucharest Jewish Press*, 1857–1994, Bucureşti, 1996, p. 58 (Iancu Gross) and 62 (S. Rivenzon). Israil Bercovici, *A hundred years of Jewish theater in Romania*, Bucureşti, 1982, p. 37 (H. St. Streitman); I. Psantir, cited work and Sam. Svemer, cited work; I. Kara, *"Reviews and studies* in "Bucareşter şriftn", vol. V, Bucureşti, 1982, p. 155– 156 (Iacob Iosef Romaner)

11. Piatra Neamţ – *Illustrated monograph*, Publishing house Cetatea Doamnei, Piatra Neamţ, 1996

    I.   Kara in "R.C.M." no. 652 / 1 Sep 1988; A.S.F.C.E.R., Register 1 / 1929, The census of the Jewish population of Roman, 1938, Extract letters I–L; Moişe Lax, cited work, p. 152 (Ronetti – Roman); Anghel Corbeanu – Max Blecher in "R.C.M 1 Jan 1972; other writers and publicists: Ira Keiss, Solomon Schoss – Roman; Leibiş Beram, Library "Rosenberg", founded from the donation of Bruno Rosenberg; "The Israelite Courier", year XII. No. 3 / 19 Sep 1920, year XIX no. 16 / 2 May1926, "The Jewish Tribune", year VI, no. 194 / 2 May 1937 (Library I Neulicht)

12. The "Rosenberg" library, which between the years 1940 and 1944 was partially part of the library of the Jewish elementary school and of the Jewish High–School of Roman, contained authors like: Eugen Relgis, Moses Schwartzfeld, Barbu Lăzăreanu, Dr. W. Filderman, Israel Zangwill, Theodor Herzl, Horia Carp, Max Nordau, Aurelian Weiss, Dr. A.D. Stern, Enric Furtună, Heinrich Heine, Eliezer Frenkel, S. Rivenzon, Bezalel Safran, H. Sanielevici.

13. "The Israelite Courier", year II, no. 22 / 7 Jun 1903, "The Opinion", Iaşi, year XVIII, no. 4511 / 11 Jun 1922, no. 39 / 28 Nov 1926

14. A.S.N.F.C.E.R., file 57 / 1942–1943

15. Archives of the Jewish community Piatra Neamţ, Register 87 / 1948

16. "The Equality", no. 21 / 30 May 1903

17. Idem, no. 29 / 25 Aug 1903, no. 46 / 26 Nov 1904

18. Idem, 24 Feb 1906, "The Israelite Courier" / 2 May 1913. "The salvation", year 2, no. 529 /3 Oct 1920; In 1920 Merlaub discussed Yohanan ben Zakai, at a meeting of Maccabi, "The rebirth," year I, no. 16 / 4 Jan 1925. In 1925, a lecture about "Chaim Nahman Bialik" was given at a Zionist meeting ("Our rebirth" / 3 Apr 1928, "The Israelite Courier" no. 1 / 4 Jan 1931)

19. "The Israelite magazine", year III, 1 Aug 1888, "Romanu", Roman / 13 Aug 1888

20. "Equality" / 4 Mar 1903, 7 May 1904

21. In 1885, theater shows were performed in a theater on Strada Mare, in the Riven houses ("The vulture" / 19 Oct 1985; "Opinion," Iaşi, year XVIII, no. 4484 / 5 May 1922)

22. "Opinion", Iaşi / 13 Mar 1928, 3 May 1928: In the third decade of the 20th century, at the Zionist section "Or Zion" an amateur group presented "Orfelina," and the Vera Kamiewska group played the operetta in 3 acts "Berele Tremp" by Aron Nagher (*History of the city of Roman*, Roman, 1992, p. 333)

23. "The Israelite Courier" / 25 Jun 1933

24. Iulian Şvarţ, *Portraits and essays* (Yidish), Bucureşti, 1981, p. 243, "The Jewish Gazette" no. 10 / 24 Apr 1942.

In addition we shall mention the musician Ignat Polydodi, born in

Kiev, and the photographers Rozenthal Solomon, Avramescu Aurel, Avramescu Josef, Schwartz Suchar and Barmack Iţic.

INDEX

Roman Memorial Book

C

H

I

J

K

L

M

T

U

V

Q

R

S

www.ingramcontent.com/pod-product-compliance
Lightning Source LLC
Chambersburg PA
CBHW080801300326
41914CB00055B/1013